IDENTITY AND SUSPICION

Being Gen 1.5 Somali Australian

Elizabeth Lakey

Connor Court Publishing

Published by Connor Court Publishing Pty Ltd, 2023

PO Box 7257
Redland Bay QLD 4165
sales@connorcourt.com
www.connorcourt.com

ISBN: 9781922815408

Cover design by Maria Giordano

Front Cover Photo: A group of African Muslim students with backpacks posing on a pink background. the concept of school education. www.shutterstock.com.

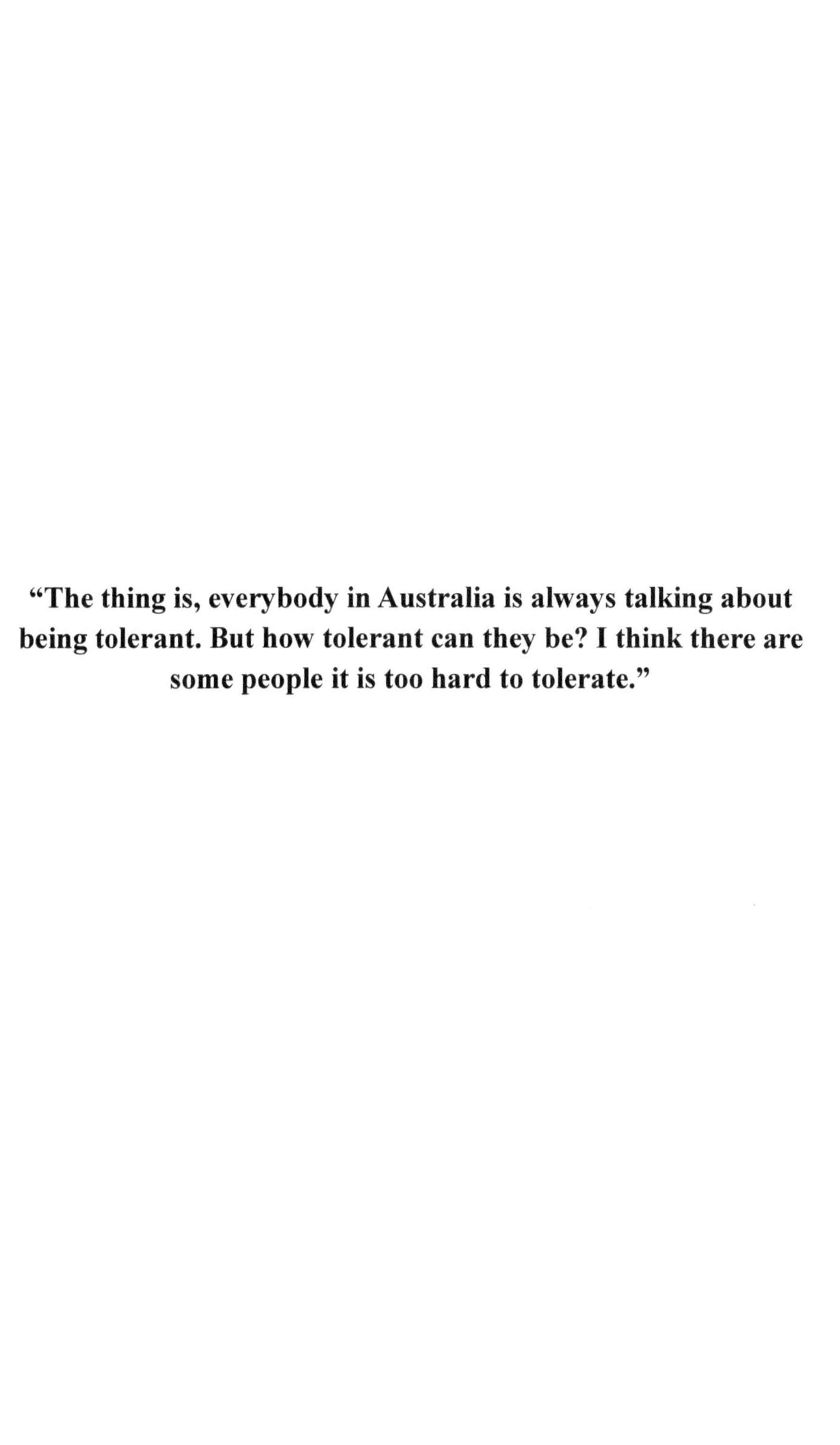

"The thing is, everybody in Australia is always talking about being tolerant. But how tolerant can they be? I think there are some people it is too hard to tolerate."

Contents

Acknowledgments 7

Foreword 9

I - Background and context

1: Migration and Melbourne – A living story 15

2: Understanding Somalia and Somalis in Melbourne 39

3: The framing of Somali identities 71

II - Gen 1.5 in their own words

4: Islam and kinship 95

5: Living under suspicion 135

6: Unique Somali ideals 177

III - Concluding reflections

7: Identity and suspicion 207

Bibliography 233

Acknowledgments

A heartfelt thank you to all those people, young and old, who generously shared their stories with me. I've changed your names here, but I remember each and every one of you.

Foreword

Dr Diana Johns

> *I'm not white, but I'm still Australian ... I feel Australian and I belong to Australia ... 'this is where I belong'* (Muna, p.16)
>
> *...we were raised here and it's normal for us... I really feel that I belong here* (Sumaya, p.166)
>
> *...getting used to two cultures and walking the fine line is not the easiest thing. ... I've found balancing the two ways, the old way and the new way can be a bit tricky at times and you have to live a double life in a sense...*" (Mansuur, p.215-6)

These are the voices and experiences of Somali Australians living in Melbourne as part of the in-between generation that Elizabeth Lakey calls "Gen 1.5" – people "born in one country and [who] have lived elsewhere from their late childhood or early teen years" (p.12). "Elsewhere" in this case is Melbourne, Australia, which is home to a small but established community of African Australians, including the predominantly Muslim Somalian community, who left their continent in the 1990s to find safety, security, and prosperity for their children. As one mother puts it:

> *We start a new life in Australia. It was difficult to get here and now we have a different future. I do not want my children to have this heavy past with them all the time.* (p.166)

Over the last decade and a half particularly, however, African Australians have been constructed as outsiders, stigmatised as Others who don't belong, and even maligned as 'criminal' threats. These representations and the misperceptions they give rise to, as Dr Lakey observes, depend largely on "what stories they [African Australians] are able to tell about themselves" (p.20). To this end, this book aims to provide a platform for "Gen 1.5 Somali Australians to use their own voices to tell their stories of the lived experience of being young, visibly different members of Australian society" (p.90).

As a criminologist my focus tends towards making sense of violence and/or the effects of criminalisation, especially involving young people. In 2016, after spending a year in Wales (UK) researching youthful 'prolific offending', I returned to Australia and was struck by how, despite African Australian communities being overwhelmingly law-abiding, heightened media attention towards any youth violence associated with African Australians cast unwarranted suspicion over an entire sector of the population. It was also striking how White voices dominated how these 'problems' were framed, in ways that seemed to drown out Black perspectives.

The media-driven 'African gangs' narrative that reached a crescendo in the lead-up to Victoria's 2018 state election, for instance, created fear and suspicion across the community and left deep scars of mistrust. This fear and suspicion had roots in political fearmongering a decade earlier, when then federal immigration minister Kevin Andrews cited concerns about South Sudanese youth 'gangs' in Victoria and their so-called difficulty in "settling and adjusting to the Australian way of life" as a justification for reducing the intake of African refugees (quoted in Farouque et al. 2007). For young people born here, in Australia, of parents who had migrated from Africa with high expectations of their children's safety, education and success, the sense of being unwelcome – of not belonging – was bewildering, angering, demoralising, hurtful.

It is scarcely surprising that many young people negotiating multiple identities – 'African', 'refugee', and Muslim – have felt as Layla did, that "I have to prove myself to so many different people" (p.196). I have heard these feelings expressed through my own work with African Australian communities. In the report, *'Don't drag me into this': Growing up South Sudanese in Victoria after the 2016 Moomba 'riot'* (Benier et al. 2018), co-produced with colleagues at Monash University and the Centre for Multicultural Youth, one participant clearly articulated this sense of having to prove themselves:

> *There are times we belong here, and there are times that we don't. And ... we don't want to belong here only when we're doing positive things. We want to belong here no matter what.* (p.2)

These examples point to the urgent need for us to listen to and centre the experiences of young people and communities affected by racist othering. To acknowledge and connect with the shared human need for belonging, and for it to be unconditional, as a matter of dignity.

And when we listen, we hear stories of fierce self-reliance, strength, and resilience: the importance of Islam and religious tradition in maintaining community cohesion, care, and reciprocity; the value placed on education; the strength and pride of Somali women, these all shine through in Lakey's account. This book thus starts to tell the "fascinating and complex story" (Lakey, p.12) of a generation caught between two cultures, Somali Gen 1.5.

Gen 1.5 is characterised by in-betweenness. Being in-between – both and neither here/there – is often a state of growth, emergence, transformation. Just as the notion of a 'third culture' generation implies *additional* rather than attenuated cultural identity, Gen 1.5 similarly evokes an extra layer of resources in the form of relational social capital. In this way, while people may be wounded or diminished by the harms of suspicion and mistrust, they can be strengthened, enlarged, and sustained by the richness of their cultural heritage, values and identity, particularly those of a people "too busy looking forward to look back" (p.229). What a wonderful, optimistic characterisation!

As a White Australian settler-occupier, I understand the apprehension about speaking *for* others, about experiences of othering. But as John A Powell articulates, there is an important *bridging* role that each of us can play in promoting belonging, and which "requires that we create space to hear and see each other" (powell, 2021). This is *a bridging story.*

References:

Benier, K, Blaustein, J, Johns, D & Maher, S (2018) Benier, K., Blaustein, J., Johns, D., & Maher, S. (2018). *'Don't drag me into this': Growing up South Sudanese in Victoria after the 2016 Moomba 'riot'.* Full report. Melbourne: Centre for Multicultural Youth.

Farouque, F, Petrie, A, & Miletic, D (2007) Minister cuts African refugee intake. *The Age*, October 2.

Powell, John A (2021) Bridging or Breaking? The Stories We Tell Will Create the Future We Inhabit. *Non-Profit Quarterly*, February 15.

I – Background and context

1

Migration and Melbourne
A living story

The seeds for this book date back to 2010, when I started tutoring Community Development at Victoria University in Footscray, in Melbourne's inner west. There were many Somali Australian students in my classes over two years, and I was struck by their decision to study community development with the explicit aim of working in their community to improve the circumstances of Somalis living in Melbourne. They were generally very studious, and often took up my offers of extra assistance outside class time. Then, when I began studying Arabic at the University of Melbourne in the following years, I met more Somali students, this time as peers, and became friends with some. We met for regular study sessions and again, I noticed how hard they worked at their studies. I began to pay more attention to the way Somalia was represented in the mainstream media and realised that the commonly available images of Somalia did not tally at all with my impressions from friends and students. This false representation had enormous impact on the young people, and the disparity between this representation and the way they saw themselves, was both enormous and damaging.

This book tells the story of a remarkable group of people living in Melbourne. After surviving natural disasters, a bloody civil war, and years in displaced persons camps, Somalis arrived in Melbourne as refugees in the mid 1990s. Many spoke no English and had lost members of their immediate and extended families. Their social ties were severed, they found themselves without any standing in society, and their qualifications were often not recognised. They had to start again from scratch, finding housing and employment, entering the education system and raising large families in small houses and apartments. Their children were often born outside Somalia, and are not familiar with the country as visits are rare or do not occur at all.

These young people are part of Somali Gen 1.5, sharing common experiences of flight and resettlement. Theirs is a fascinating and complex story, which this book starts to tell. Gen 1.5 are individuals who were born in one country and have lived elsewhere from their late childhood or early teen years. This means they have cultural understanding of both their (or their parents' if the Gen 1.5 individual was born outside Somalia) country of birth and the place they now call home. They have been raised to have pride in their Somali heritage, despite the negative perception of Somalia in the broader community. They are often 'caught in the middle' between two cultures. They bring cultural understanding of Somalia, and they have lived much of their lives in Australia, which places them half way between first and second generation migrants. Practically, this might mean translating for their parents, or making appointments and navigating bureaucracy as their parents have difficulty understanding the way Australian systems work. However, this straddling of cultures also has many abstract and emotional facets. Specifically, young Somali Australians in Melbourne occupy contested identities. In the family sphere, they battle with competing parental and peer group expectations. In the religious sphere, they describe tension between their faith and the expectations of mainstream Australians. In the public sphere, they have been raised in an environment where there is widespread and increasing distrust of Muslims and people who are visibly different.

Individuals and groups inhabit many different identities over space and time, and tell stories about themselves to reinforce those identities. In a migrant nation like Australia, the question of identity takes on heightened significance. The migration story in Australia is a living story, and it is in constant flux. Melbourne is a city where many cultures and worldviews exist side-by-side. The expression and intersection of this cultural manifestation is captivating and sometimes tense to observe and take part in. In some ways, this is also a generic story. People who arrive and settle in another place are often confronted with disadvantage, misunderstandings, and a struggle to have their own cultural practices accepted. And the next generation is forced to negotiate with an added layer of complexity because they are at the forefront of managing and negotiating identities that come from different places — geographical, cultural and perhaps imagined.

Somalia is a country with a troubled political history. After being colonised in the late 19th century by Italy and Britain, the former-colonial regions joined forces to create the Independent Somali Republic in 1960. When Mohamed Siyad Barre who had seized power in 1969 and founded the Somali Democratic Republic was overthrown, violent civil war broke out. After the eruption of war, waves of refugees fled the country. They have settled in many parts of the world, most notably in Sweden and greater Scandinavia, Minnesota in the United States, Canada and the United Kingdom. There is also a small but significant population in Australia.

While the size of the Somali community in Melbourne is not large compared to other Somali diaspora communities (especially in the United States), there has been substantial media focus on Horn of Africa populations in Melbourne, and indeed on the Somali community in particular. Somalis are African and almost exclusively

Muslim. Muslim communities across the globe are no strangers to hyperbolic representation, and Somalis have been characterised as violent in both academic literature and the popular and mainstream media. This book seeks to give Somali Gen 1.5 a chance to answer some of the charges laid against them. Their identity expression is vastly different to the way it is commonly represented: this generation of Somalis seems no more likely to engage in violent behaviour than the average Australian of the same age. However, when violence does occur, it is subject to much more scrutiny than when it occurs in a mainstream setting. Within the community there are mixed reactions to the media scrutiny. There are those who welcome the media attention because it draws attention to Somalis in Melbourne, one Somali community leader explained. This in turn could highlight the work that many of their community organisations do. He hoped this might also lead to social, multicultural, and educational programs developed and targeted at the Somali community. However, many of the young people felt very differently. They believed they were targeted unfairly by the media and indeed were profoundly affected by their representation in the media.

Some of the young people felt that they did not have a space to tell their stories, and so I spent three years between 2012-2015 getting to know some young Somali-Australians. I went to cultural events, graduation celebrations, and met some of the many formidable Somali-Australian community leaders. I also conducted a series of interviews and focus groups with young people where we enjoyed wide-ranging discussions that touched on life in Melbourne, family responsibilities, religion and educational and career aspirations. What emerged was a picture of an extraordinarily resilient community, where many voices are raised in advocacy, and groups have formed to address community needs. The young people have a unique perspective on their place in the Somali and Australian community, and I have tried to give them space to tell their stories in their own words.

◊

One topic that was enduring in many conversations with the young people was the notion of 'feeling at home'.

> ***Amal**: Once I got over not knowing English, my primary school years up to year 7 or 8, I didn't feel any different. You know, even with my scarf, I didn't pay any attention to it at all. It was just in high school when I felt myself growing apart from my parents and I couldn't speak to them. And later, in year 12, people started looking, and making comments.*

Amal touches on many important issues. The forging of her identity, her status as Gen 1.5, being different from her parents, the importance of language as a normalising discursive structure, the 'look' of others who started to see her in terms of ideological categories and the power relations in such moves. Everything here centres on the theme of identity and just how challenged this space is for Amal. While Amal discusses the challenges that come with being part of a visibly different migrant community, she also talks about what it means to be a young person and the act of defining oneself differently from parents. This is a core part of maturing and becoming an adult, and in some ways is a very normal story. However, for Amal, and many other young people across Melbourne, this already confusing time is further complicated by the varying expectations they face in terms of family, ethnic, and mainstream identity.

> ***Sumaya**: Australia has the same values as I have, Islamically and culturally. It's universal values. So I don't feel like I don't belong. It's my home. I don't think I'll ever go back to Somalia. I know there are people who dream of going back, but I'll never go back there, I don't think it would be safe to live there. This is my home; my grandchildren are going to be born here. So I feel that my identity is Australian.*

Sumaya is decisive in stating that she feels Australian. She, like many Gen 1.5 young people I spoke to, repeated that she feels Australian through and through. However, I was struck by the language they often used. Sumaya highlights this for us in stating that she feels Australian. Note that she does not claim that she *is* Australian. This distinction, while small, is also very telling. I have never heard similar language from young Australians who don't belong to a recently arrived migrant community. Sumaya also presents her identity against the backdrop of the harsh reality that for reasons of personal safety, she could not return to Somalia, even if she wanted to. This was a common theme in our discussions, as relatives still in Somalia described a situation where there were intermittent curfews, political instability and regular cuts to water and power supplies. So for many of the young people, regardless of whether they 'felt at home', there was very little alternative to living in Australia.

> ***Muna**: The first time I went to Malaysia, a taxi driver asked me and I told him I'm Australian. That was the first thing that came out of my mouth, I didn't really think about it. It just came out. And he said 'You're not Australian, you're not white.' And I thought... 'No, I'm not white, but I'm still Australian.' But I didn't say it out loud. I was thinking it, but I didn't say it. As soon as he said, 'You're not Australian', I jumped and said, 'Oh, I'm Somali'. But in my mind... I'm not Australian, but I feel Australian and I belong to Australia, but the second thing that came out was I'm Somali, even though I don't really believe that. But... when I came back [from travel] and thought 'this is where I belong.'*

Muna's story highlights how contested the question of identity is, both for members of Gen 1.5, and in terms of other individuals' projections of categories of identity. Like Sumaya (and the majority of the other young people I got to know), she explicitly states that she is 'not Australian', but that she 'feels Australian'. She draws a distinction between her feeling of being Australian, and her capacity to call herself truly Australian. These comments reveal much about the importance of a sense of belonging, and in probing deeper, it became clear that the feelings of unease about belonging were present for Gen 1.5 in their sense of identity, and in their everyday lives in Melbourne. They shoulder a unique burden in that they live between cultures. The way in which this group creates, maintains and expresses identity is a fascinating study of youth agency and resilience.

In the face of complex and competing claims on their identity, young Somalis living in Melbourne express themselves in a myriad of complex and contested ways. This all takes place in an intricate space with multiple competing social forces, as well as a deep engagement with Islam. The young people actively negotiate this space with an acute awareness of how their identities are represented. This is not an abstract awareness, but one that shapes their approach to life and permeates everyday interactions.

◊

Gen 1.5 Somalis in Australia share a particular way of being in the world; a history, culture and context, which demarcates them from others. This shared horizon has been termed 'generation 1.5'. The term 'generation 1.5' was initially used in the 1980s to describe immigrant youth who were not born in the United States. However, since Rumbaut and Ima's initial use of the label, educators and researchers have used the name in varying ways (Frodesen 2002).

Here is Rumbaut and Ima's (1988) description of their target population from the first pages of their seminal manuscript addressing generation 1.5:

> These respondents are members of what we will call the "1.5" generation: that is, they are neither part of the "first" generation of their parents, the responsible adults who were formed in the homeland, who made the fateful decision to leave it and to flee as

> refugees to an uncertain exile in the United States [...] nor are the youths part of the "second" generation of children who are born in the U.S., and for whom the "homeland" exists as a representation consisting of parental memories and memorabilia, even though their ethnicity may remain well-defined. Rather, the refugee youths in our study constitute a distinctive cohort: they are those young people who were born in their countries of origin but formed in the U.S.; [. . .] they were not the main protagonists of the decision to leave and hence are less beholden to their parents' attitudes [. . .]; and they are in many ways marginal to both the new and old worlds, for while they straddle both worlds they are in some sense fully part of neither of them. [. . .] Though they differ greatly from each other in cultural and social class origins, [. . .] they generally share a common psychohistorical location in terms of their age and migration status/role, and in terms of developing bicultural strategies of response and adjustment to that unique position which they occupy as "1.5'ers" in the interstices, as it were, of two societies and cultures, between the first and second generation, between being "refugees" and being "ethnics" (or "hyphenated Americans") (Rumbaut and Ima 1988, 1-2).

In these, the first observations where generation 1.5 was named, the key characteristic of this group is their inability to identify fully with either their immigrant parents' generation or their own American peers. 'They occupied a nebulous space between two different cultures' (Huster 2011, 7-8).

This is not to say that this is the first instance of researchers investigating such a group of people. Indeed, there have been countless studies of such people with almost identical descriptions, that do not use the term 'generation 1.5'. In fact, one could argue that practically any description of migrant communities will include groups of young individuals who feel 'caught in the middle' between two cultures, as there are always children involved in migration flows (Watson 1977; Pinchbeck and Hewitt 1973). Nevertheless, a technical term was coined in 1988 for a pre-existing phenomenon, and the concept has gained traction.

Oudenhoven described the generation 1.5 Latino students that she studied as being 'caught in the middle' (Oudenhoven 2006). The members of generation 1.5 are often described as straddling the gulf between nations, languages, cultures, religions, and more. There is a powerful metaphor in the use of the verb 'caught' because the generation 1.5 is indeed unable to choose one side of the gulf over the other. Their identity is formed and held over that space and it is difficult to jump (either back and forth, or permanently to one side). The terminology used when describing generation 1.5 usually refers to their unstable and uncertain identity (Huster 2011). While many studies of generation 1.5 in various settings and circumstances point out the negative aspects of being caught in the middle, there is also undoubtedly a positive side to the equation. Some of the young people I spoke to enjoyed helping their parents make sense of Australian mainstream culture. Others were proud of their own ability to understand different ways of life. Still more emphasised how lucky they were to speak their language of origin as well as English.

While studies of generation 1.5 migrants have highlighted their difficulty identifying with either their parents' culture or the culture of their new homeland, this does not suggest that this question is easy to navigate for other migrants and refugees. In focussing on the specific challenges faced by generation 1.5ers I do not wish to imply that other individuals occupy a monoculture and do not have to deal with similar issues. All social actors occupy contested identities, and indeed, there is no monoculture that generation 1.5 can be positioned against. However, generation 1.5 have been identified as having salient traits that position them apart from other groups.

◊

At a time of increasing parochialism and untruths in politics and many sections of the media, it is especially important to tell the stories of people who have been marginalised, or who are considered to be on the outer edges of society. For some years there has been, at least periodically, strong interest in African Australians within Australia, with consistent reportage using emotive language such as 'African Gangs', 'radicalised youths' and Islamic 'terror cells' in the popular media. Australia is certainly not alone in this regard. Increased nationalism across Europe and North America is matched by the rise of far-right parties and unrest in parts of Latin America. There is a strong temptation to turn inward and a heightened sense of difference between ethnic, religious, political and other groups. It has never been more crucial to talk to people of different colours and creeds, and to step outside our own narrow perspectives to really try to hear others and see things from their points of view. This is increasingly difficult to do among the clamorous voices from many quarters, and the current global circumstances where a pandemic is politicised and blame is laid on human actors rather than an entirely impassive virus, is testament to increasing global polarisation and division. Increased political instability, the changing climate, poverty and conflict continue to force flight and migration from many areas, and human movement under these circumstances is dangerous and sometimes fatal.

Where a group of migrants or refugees establishes a community, they likely face an uphill battle to settle, gain access to the labour market, education, and many other services. Their reception by the host community is highly dependent on how they are represented by local media, and what stories they are able to tell about themselves. All of this is true for the Somali community in Melbourne, and this book is a small attempt to correct the balance and allow a platform for Gen 1.5 Somali Australians to speak for themselves. While the media might focus on the perceived inability of refugees and migrants to integrate into a host culture, anthropologists have long moved away from the concept of cultures clashing, preferring to examine dynamic lived experiences that speak to emergence and transformation. There is a strong body of literature examining the receiving of migrants and refugees internationally. This book aims to build on this scholarly tradition, and explores the way children of refugees who are visibly different from the host society population navigate their allegiances to their culture of origin and the culture of their everyday circumstances in a receiving society.

◊

This book is divided into three main sections. The first of these covers the context for the work and includes three chapters. A recent history of migration to Australia is presented, with a focus on Muslim migration, the events that shape the reasons for migration, and the difficulties encountered in settlement. The next section seeks to contextualise both Somalia and the Somali people living in Melbourne. It examines the 'official' version of Somali history, and then takes a closer look at some contested issues. The third chapter provides specific historical and political circumstances and demographic information about the community in Melbourne, before a grounding in identity theories most relevant to Gen 1.5 Somalis in Melbourne is provided. Drawing on a number of scholars' work, the core argument is that individuals may inhabit numerous, dynamic and fluid identities. The immense importance that the political notion of power has in the construction and expression of identity is highlighted. Issues surrounding the conceptualisation of identity, power and social capital are also covered. Identity is formed and expressed in complex interaction with social norms and expectations. The concept of social capital is used to explore how these interactions take place. Finally, the concept of Gen 1.5 is examined briefly, followed by an explanation of how this conception fits the young Somali Australians who shared their stories in this study.

Section two of the book also comprises three chapters, which provide insights from the research through the words of Somali Gen 1.5 themselves. The first chapter focuses on two important facets of Somali life: Islam as part of the lived experience, and their perceptions of the clan system and notions of kinship. A distinction is drawn between the ways Gen 1.5 engage with Islam in a very practical sense (observing dietary requirements, daily prayers, regular worship) and the way that their knowledge of the clan system, while quite sophisticated, is mostly theoretical, and not part of everyday practice. The next chapter explores what it means to live under suspicion, both in terms of how Gen 1.5 experience and interpret acts of violence committed by or against members of their community, and in the steps they take to protect themselves in the face of public misrepresentations. The final chapter in this section discusses two uniquely Somali ideals that distinguish them from other Muslim and Horn of Africa migrant communities in Melbourne. The first is the value placed on education in the Somali community and the perspectives of Gen 1.5 on the importance of education. Education is highly prized by the Somali Australian community, and consequently carries a great deal of expectation. The second is the esteemed place of women in the Somali community and their power and agency in both the domestic and public spheres.

The conclusion reflects on the complex and contested sphere of identity expression that Gen 1.5 Somali Australians must master. The study discusses radicalisation and focuses on how fear of young practicing Muslims affects their engagement with the broader community. A reflection on how remarkable these young people are as they negotiate significant barriers to expressing their identity follows. These barriers are both visible and invisible and permeate every aspect of life. Finally, some further avenues of research are recommended.

◊

There are some limitations to this research. These centre on the small sample size of the population, and the inability to draw quantitative conclusions from this sample. However, it is well understood that deep qualitative data collected from a small sample provides different insight to other forms of data. This study has engaged with a small number of young Somali Australians in order to hear from them in their own words, and to empower them to speak for themselves.

Another limitation to consider is the dilemma of being a researcher that is not part of the community. This has benefits as well as disadvantages. While there are some cultural aspects it will be very difficult for an external researcher to fully understand, there is also a freedom in terms of the research participants being able to speak more openly, without fear of repercussion or judgement which may be the result of speaking with a community member.

◊

Human history has been characterised by the movement of people, from the initial migration of homo sapiens out of East Africa, to the flows of the present day motivated by conflict, the search for economic prosperity, and the changing climate. These patterns of relocation have varied widely, from migrations in the period of early sedentary agriculture (around 10,000 BCE) to the movements around the Mediterranean Mesopotamian and Roman worlds, to the far-reaching phenomenon of successive waves of Western colonisation, and finally, the aftermath of decolonisation in the recent past.

The most recent era of migration arguably began in the 1950s with the wave of decolonisation sweeping across many previously colonial territories (Harzig, Hoerder, and Gabaccia 2009, 45). The colonial beginnings to white settlement in Australia were characterised by brutal treatment of the indigenous population, who were stripped of their lands, rights, and humanity. Australia has a discreditable past in terms of who has been allowed and encouraged to migrate, and who has been barred from entry, or forcibly removed.

After the Second World War the global driver of migration was essentially the Western demand for labour (Castles and Miller 2008, 91). Flows of people moved largely from the South to the North (from developing countries to more developed countries), attracted by the prospects of better living standards. Other migrants from former colonies moved to countries like Britain, France and The Netherlands. Circumstances were different in North America and Australia, where labour was required to support economic development but also to increase populations. Indeed, in both the years 1949 and 1950, approximately 150,000 people migrated to Australia, bringing the total migration to Australia in the post-war years to around half a million people (Phillips and Klapdor 2010, 15). While the Australian indigenous population has lived on the continent for many thousands of years, and is considered the longest continual culture in the world, replete with rich traditions and oral history, Australia is often described as a 'migrant nation' partly because of this increase in migration after the Second World War.

At the time, migrants generally moved on a permanent basis and those who were deemed to possess the right characteristics enjoyed broad civic rights. Under the 'White Australia' scaffold, European migrants were preferred, with as many British as possible, because other newcomers would bring 'imported' cultures that were different from locally produced 'Australian' cultures (notwithstanding the *extreme* newness of the recently imported local Australian culture in direct opposition to the many thousands of years of continuous indigenous culture) (Carter 2006, 71). However, by the 1960s, the urgent need for migrant labour had broadened the eligibility criteria for those allowed to enter the country. Many European Muslims, mainly people from Turkey, took advantage of these opportunities to seek a new life in Australia. There was an agreement between the Turkish and Australian governments between 1967 and 1971 under which approximately 10,000 Turkish citizens settled in Australia (Saeed 2004, 7). In the 1970s, many Lebanese citizens also settled in Australia, with Lebanon becoming one of the top 10 countries of origin for the overseas-born population in Australia by the 1981 census (Phillips and Klapdor 2010, 23). This is not to suggest that the waves of Muslims that arrived in the 1960s and 1970s were the same as those who followed in later decades. Indeed, Turkish and Lebanese Muslims are distinct from Muslims from Africa or South-East Asia (for example). Nevertheless, this is the first example of significant numbers of Muslims migrating to Australia.

Muslims in Australia have a rich history which may pre-date European settlement. Some of Australia's earliest visitors were Muslim, from the east Indonesian archipelago. They are thought to have made contact with the Indigenous population of mainland Australia as early as the 16th and 17th centuries. Muslim presence in Australia has been recorded since the 1800s. The first arrivals were Afghan camel drivers who worked in the vast and arid desserts inland. The Ghan railway from Adelaide to Darwin is named in their honour. Many of these Asians (almost always called 'Afghans', despite their varied origins) settled around Alice Springs and in areas of the Northern Territory. The first mosque in Australia was built at Maree in South Australia in 1861 (Australian Government 2009). Under the White Australia policy, non-European Muslim migrants were denied entry in the early 20th century, however, Muslims of European descent were permitted to enter the country. Interestingly, this manifestly unjust social policy made a distinction between different sorts of Muslims based on ethnic grounds. This saw a small wave of Albanian Muslims arrive in the 1920s and another one after the Second World War. Shepparton in Victoria, where the first Albanian mosque was built in 1960, became a hub for the Victorian Albanian Muslim community and is now a regional hub for Sudanese migrants (Mehmet 2009).

In line with the general increase of Australia's population following the Second World War, the Muslim population also increased significantly. This was largely due to the post–war economic boom, which created new employment opportunities. While Melbourne's ethnic diversity had until recently been largely Europe-based, a significant wave of migrants from south-east and northern Asia arrived throughout the 1970s. In the last three decades, many Muslims have come to Australia under migration and humanitarian programs.

In the post-war years, the Australian government actively engaged in a program to significantly increase the country's population rapidly. Under the (rather ominous) slogan 'Populate or Perish!', it invited millions of migrants and displaced persons from Europe. Multiculturalism was adopted as the official government policy in the 1970s, and the White Australia restrictions were finally reversed (Australian Government 2014). This significantly broadened the eligibility criteria for migrants and consequently, there was an influx of migrants who had not been previously permitted entry to Australia. This included Lebanese Muslims (and Lebanese Christians), and Muslims from Africa, South East and Central Asia and from the Middle East.

In the late 1970s, the first Vietnamese 'boat people' began to arrive in Australia. They were fleeing the war in their homeland and their arrival coincided with a period of social change and upheaval in Australia. There was much popular opposition to the Vietnam war, and the refugees were welcomed to Australia. Since then, there have been successive waves of sea-borne refugees, from China, Chile and most recently from Sri Lanka, Africa and the Middle East (Australian Government 2013). However, it has only been in more recent years that significant numbers of Muslim refugees have begun to attempt the risky passage to Australia by boat. This has been a direct response to the conflicts that have plagued countries like Syria, Iraq and Afghanistan for the last decades.

After the September 11, 2001 attacks in America, the security of Australian borders became linked to terrorism in every day political and media discourse (although boat arrivals were not linked to terrorist attacks in any way previously) (Australian Government 2013). The then Defence Minister Peter Reith warned that unauthorised arrival by boat could be 'a pipeline for terrorists to come in and use your country as a staging post for terrorist activities' (MacLellan 2002, 147). The vast majority of asylum seekers arrive in Australia by plane rather than boat (between 2015 and 2020, fewer than 500 people arrived in Australia by boat, although this period coincides with the federal government policy of forcibly turning boats back (Refugee Council 2021)). However, this equation of boat people with terrorism is still prevalent, and has also been linked to Islam, and remains a strong belief in some quarters of the Australian population.

Recent decades have seen upheaval across many different areas of the Muslim world. Conflict and tensions remain high in many regions resulting in extraordinary levels of displacement. Following the U.S. military occupation of Iraq, the country continues to face large-scale displacement and pressing humanitarian needs. Millions of Iraqis fled their homes and still live in desperate circumstances (Refugees International 2011a). Similarly, the ethnic violence in Darfur and South Sudan has displaced millions (Refugees International 2011b). In Palestine, it is estimated that up to 7.2 million people have been displaced as a result of the ongoing political stalemate in the region (Institute for Middle East Understanding 2009). In 2010, the Brookings Institute calculated that there were nine to ten million refugees in the Muslim world and at least

14 million internally displaced people (Amr and Ferris 2010). With the ongoing Syrian refugee crisis, this has increased considerably.

At the 2016 Census 604,200 people self-identified as Muslims in Australia, which accounts for 2.6% of the total Australian population. This represents an increase of 15% from the 2011 census, when 476,291 people identified as Muslims in Australia, most likely due to relatively high birth and immigration rates (particularly from South Asia). At first glance an increase of 15% over a period of only four years seems large for any demographic group, however during the same period of time, other minority religions in Australia including Hinduism and Buddhism also increased quite substantially in size. Predominantly concentrated in Sydney and Melbourne, Australia's Muslim communities make up a small, but culturally diverse section of Australian society (Phillips 2007). However, there is a great deal of misunderstanding about Australia's Muslim population. Muslim Australians are not a homogeneous group as some media reports might lead us to believe.

Muslims in Australia are subjected to a very high level of media scrutiny and reporting (Peucker, Roose, and Akbarzadeh 2014). This scrutiny often produces shallow and simplistic reportage (Ghauri and Umber 2019). Over the last two decades in Australia, there has been an extreme awareness of 'boat people' and fears about terrorism, which have been actively linked not only by unscrupulous media outlets, but also by the general press and by government ministers. Issues surrounding terrorism, radicalised Islamic youth, and concerns regarding Muslim assimilation are present in the public discourse. Although the Muslim population of Australia is relatively small (<3%) it receives a statistically disproportionate amount of media attention. Most of this attention is negative (Akbarzadeh and Smith 2005). For example, one journalist in The Australian has described Muslim migration as a 'huge, unregulated Islamic inflow'. He believes that 'this boatpeople phenomenon is essentially a determined Muslim immigration' (Sheridan 2013).

In the context of vocal debates around migration to Australia and the capacity of already stretched infrastructure to meet the needs of new migrants, the consistent media reports discussing violence committed by youths 'of African appearance', and the regular speculation around radicalisation in Muslim communities, it is fair to say that the majority of public messages around Islam in Australia is overwhelmingly negative (Akbarzadeh and Smith 2005; Dixon and Williams 2015; Sian, Law, and Sayyid 2012). It is often forgotten in Australia that there is a largely peaceful Muslim world at our doorstep. Many of our closest neighbours are Islamic countries or have significant numbers of Muslim inhabitants. Islam is the second largest of the world's religions, and while Islam in the popular imagination, and often in the media, is disproportionately identified with the Arab world, the vast majority of Muslims live in Asia and Africa (Esposito 2008, 3).

◊

In recent years, Islam has become an area of intense scholarly interest with numerous studies exploring various aspects of the belief system and its followers in the Australian and indeed wider Western contexts. One common theme of these studies has been media coverage (Kabir 2006; Akbarzadeh and Smith 2005; Manning 2004). Another area of interest is the relationship between Australian democracy and Islam (Poynting and Mason 2006; Saeed 2003), and, of course, terrorism (Spalek and Imtoual 2007). While considerable academic efforts have sought to illustrate the homogenisation of Muslim identity in dominant discourse, there is a need for scholarship that engages with specific ethnic and cultural Muslim communities. This will help to avoid the continued homogenisation of Muslim identity and contribute to a greater understanding of the richness and depth of cultural and religious practice of Muslims in Australia today.

Over the past decade an extensive compendium of literature on Islamic identity has been compiled across a variety of intellectual fields. A significant portion of this research seeks to examine young Muslims born and raised in western contexts, the types of identities they exhibit, and the many and varied influences on their identity construction and manifestation (Pregulman and Burke 2012; Perrie and Minteh 2014). What these studies have shown most clearly is that there is a plethora of possible ways of 'being Muslim' and also that there is no one cohesive Muslim identity with which academics and social commentators may engage (Yazbeck Haddad and Smith 2002).

Much of the literature concerning Muslims living in non-Muslim majority communities is focused on issues around the concept of identity. In a study of young British Muslim women, Claire Dwyer states that it is important to understand the many subject positions young Muslims occupy as well as the 'extent to which their everyday lives are constituted in and through matrices of power embedded in intersecting discourses and material practices' (Dwyer 1998). While this is necessarily true of subjects in a society, Dwyer highlights the magnitude of this for young Muslims compared with other groups.

One important aspect of identity for Gen 1.5 is that, as a result of rapidly developing technology, and the effects of globalisation. There are myriad ways to stay connected, even with a country that has been in political turmoil for more than two decades. Somalis in Australia can contact friends and family in Somalia using various forms of technology and, until the COVID 19 pandemic closed Australia's borders, could fly back home if desired. Perhaps equally importantly, they can access international and local news in a language of their choice and can communicate their own news and information to members of their community, in Australia, in Somalia, and elsewhere around the world.

The ease of transnational communications has allowed young Somalis to create their identities in Australia, but with some reinforcement from Somalia and Somalis elsewhere. It provides them with a direct line to the prevalent cultural, social and religious ideals in Somalia, despite the thousands of kilometres that separate their new home from their old home. There are many blogs and forums dedicated to young people's experience of Somali life outside Somalia. This is a relatively new phenomenon in the refugee experience, as in the past refugees might go for years or even decades without consistent communication from their birth country. This aspect of technology was also often a topic of discussion in interviews and focus groups.

While in academia, and in the public discourse Islam is most often discussed as a political and religious phenomenon, it is often forgotten that it is, of course, also a social phenomenon. The outward expression of Islam in society is deeply embedded in the actions of its practitioners. In the current complex politico-social context, it is imperative to understand why and how people are configuring who they are in relation to Islam.

Reporting on Muslims and Islam is a staple for most forms of media. Some recurrent themes are: Islamic radicalisation and the threat of terrorism; an Islamic war against the West; civil wars in a number of Muslim majority countries and the associated displacement— refugee camps with tents as far as the eye can see, women and children bearing arms to protect their meagre possessions as they flee and the emptiness of towns that have been ransacked and looted.

There is a constant debate around democratisation in the Islamic world. Some commentators believe the process, while messy, is underway, beginning with the Arab Spring of 2011-12. Others mourn that this revolution was stifled and not able to reach its potential. This constant attention plays into a cycle where migrant and refugee Muslims are subjected to a very high level of media scrutiny, shallow and simplistic reportage, with many 'sound-bite characterisations' of Muslims which play to a sensationalist agenda perpetuated not only by the media but also politicians. Issues surrounding terrorism, radicalised Islamic youth, and concerns regarding Muslim assimilation receive high levels of public attention. In Australia, these issues are often at the forefront of Australian politics and foreign policy, and more recently, many Muslims in Melbourne have felt victimised by media coverage suggesting they have behaved irresponsibly and allowed the spread of COVID 19 (Renaldi 2020). There is also heightened interest in the wives and children of Islamic State fighters who are now living in Syrian refugee camp. Despite many of these women and children having Australian citizenship, and living in difficult conditions, there is no move from the Government to bring them home.

Many young people I spoke with told me they were concerned that when there are raids on Muslims in connection with terrorism, these are often televised and highly reported, but in the end, many of the accused have cases dismissed against them, which is not widely reported at all. When Islam is mentioned in popular discourse in Australia, it is often in the context of terrorism, conflict, and failure to integrate. This is in part due to the media's traditional reliance on conflict to tell a story. While there is some balanced reporting on Muslim communities in Australia, Islam is often conceived of as a monolith. The reality is, of course that there are many different Muslim communities in Australia, coming from all over the world, and practicing Islam in different ways. This book is focussed on one Muslim community in Melbourne, and I begin by turning my attention to their elusive and complex homeland: Somalia.

2

Understanding Somalia and Somalis in Melbourne

The Federal Republic of Somalia is a young nation state. It was proclaimed in Mogadishu on 1 July 1960 when the previously Italian-administered territory of Somalia achieved independence and merged with the former British protectorate which had become independent just four days earlier. The history of the region and the Somali people however stretches back over many centuries.

The Kingdom of Punt, as described in ancient Egyptian writings, was probably located in the area of Somalia's northern and eastern coastlines. Trading routes were established in these areas between the 7th and 10th centuries AD and Somali nomads have lived in the interior of these areas since this time. As Somalis migrated east and south, they expelled or absorbed the Oromo pastoralists and Bantu farming peoples and took over coastal towns that had belonged to the Swahili people of East Africa including Mogadishu.

There are varied theories about the beginnings of Islam in Somalia. It is thought that early in the Prophet's ministry, a band of persecuted Muslims fled across the Red Sea into the Horn of Africa with the Prophet's encouragement. There the Muslims were afforded protection by the Ethiopian Negus. Alternatively, Islam could have come to Somalia via contacts with Persian and Arab merchants and seamen who founded settlements along the Somali coast more than one thousand years ago.

Today the Somali people occupy the republic created in 1960, and also the Hawd and Ogaden regions of eastern Ethiopia, southern Djibouti, and north-eastern Kenya. Until the colonial period of the 1840s, the Somali people had never formed a single political unit. Rather, their organisation was based on clan and region. With the 'scramble for Africa' in the late 19th century, Somali borders were drawn with European interests as the primary concern. Even so, it is widely argued that Somali homogeneity is reinforced by a 'profound adherence to Islam' (Barrows 2008), and by cultural, linguistic and ethnic unity, which will be explored in further detail.

◊

Somalia has a long history of colonial involvement, much of it concerned with the territorial ambitions of both the colonisers and the indigenous population. At the turn of the 16th century, Somali armies invaded Abyssinia, with Ottoman support. They destroyed many historic buildings, churches and manuscripts during this campaign. The use of firearms, which were only seldom available in Abyssinia at that time contributed to the conquest of significant territories (Pankhurst 1998, 90). The Abyssinians were saved by the arrival of a Portuguese expedition to help their fellow Christians (Prestage 1933). Hostilities continued for the remainder of the century. This likely influenced the development of a close relationship between the Somalis and the Ottomans, which subsequently kept the geopolitical tensions high in the area.

Centuries later, both British and Italian colonial involvement with Somalia was commercially motivated, with the British garrison at Aden establishing relations with northern Somali coastal towns in order to secure a reliable source of supplies. Italian involvement in

Somalia began in 1888 when an Italian political figure, Vincenzo Filonardi, leased several coastal towns from the Sultan of Zanzibar. When his companies failed, the Italian state assumed control in 1905 (Barrows 2008). The French controlled what is now Djibouti, where people of Somali ethnic origins still live today.

Colonial intervention in the early to mid-19th century drastically altered the political, cultural and economic Somali context. The country was considered strategically valuable, but with limited economic potential (Samatar 1989). Colonial powers developed some infrastructure, such as the Franco-Ethiopian railway, and ports in coastal towns, however the colonial division of Somalia has had profoundly negative consequences, perhaps chiefly in the contested borders. When the Italians (briefly) occupied Ethiopia (1935-1936), they attached the ethnically Somali regions of Ogaden and Hawd to the colonial Somali province. However, when England restored Ethiopia's independence, the borders with Ethiopia were re-established, dividing ethnic Somalis. Territorial change and ambition are two defining factors in Somali political history. Conflicts such as the 1977-78 attack on Ethiopia weakened the regime of Muhammad Siyad Barre, and preceded a decade of instability before the eventual outbreak of civil war in 1991.

◊

The period immediately after the achievement of independence in 1960 was one of relative peace. Indeed, the Somali Republic was celebrated by many as having a particularly strong potential to become an enduring state in the sub-Saharan African context. Scholars referenced the ethnic, linguistic, religious and cultural homogeneity as evidence for this belief. Somalia was described as a 'nation in search of a state'. However, clan-based political fragmentation escalated as dozens of clan-based parties formed (Besteman 1999, 12). The 1969 elections (only nine years post-independence), saw

64 parties contesting to represent a population of less than four million. It is possible that these parties represented clan lines rather than political ideologies (Samatar 1988).

Weak and uneven economic development of the country during this period, coupled with the political ambitions of different clans eventually led to the assassination of the president, Abdirashid Ali Shermarka and a coup d'état by the army chief of staff, General Muhammad Siyad Barre on 21 October 1969 (Barrows 2008).

One of Barre's great aims was to foster a sense of nationalist identity through 'scientific socialism'. Some of his policies were quite liberal, such as those which allowed women greater rights and outlawed female infibulation (Besteman 1999, 13). However, much of his policy focused on outlawing traditional practice at the stroke of a pen. In a common nation-building move, to encourage greater loyalty to the state and law, Barre created government bodies to punish disloyalty under the National Security Laws of 1970 (Besteman 1999, 12). Tribalism and lack of revolutionary zeal were considered disloyalty (Lewis 2002, 212), and a number of detractors who spoke out against the regime were publicly executed (Ingiriis 2010). Initially, Siyad Barre enjoyed a great deal of support. However, he was ultimately unable to provide a solution to Somalia's political instability, and Somalis remained divided along lineage lines, despite his efforts at unification (Besteman 1999).

In 1970, President Barre declared Somalia a socialist state, greatly strengthening relations with the USSR. In 1977, with the help of Soviet arms, Somalia attempted to seize the Ogaden region of Ethiopia, but was defeated. The tables turned when the USSR switched its allegiance to Ethiopia, based on the socialist orientation of the new Ethiopian administration. Consequently, Somalia improved its relations with its Arab neighbours and the United States, completing the turnaround between global powers.

Barre's regime was weakened considerably by his unsuccessful territorial ambitions regarding Ethiopia. Increasing corruption, coupled with a crippling drought inland, led to a group of local clan leaders finally deposing him in 1991. At this tumultuous time, British Somaliland also seceded from Somalia. A new leader could not be agreed upon and the ensuing power struggle between clan leaders Mohamed Farah Aideed and Ali Mahdi Mohamed killed and wounded thousands of civilians.

◊

Since the outbreak of war in 1991, Somalia has periodically witnessed intense conflict between insurgent groups, with refugees fleeing advancing fronts from many directions. By 1992, some six million people were facing starvation and the UN deployed troops against rival warlords throughout the country. Following this outbreak of anarchy, Somali factions participated in conferences in neighbouring countries and elsewhere under the auspices of the UN and the African Union. Attempts at unification came close to success in 2002, although the new president and parliament (elected and convened in Kenya) were prevented from moving to Mogadishu by hostile factions.

There has followed a string of transitional governments, with many rounds of peace talks and multiple international interventions. The Transitional Federal Government was established in 2004. However, conflict continued to escalate, with the administration's Prime Minister narrowly avoiding death in an attack in 2005. In 2006 the Transitional Federal Government regained the South of Somalia from the Islamic Courts Union. The Islamic Courts Union then splintered into various radical groups, perhaps most notably Al Shabaab. These groups have since been fighting the Somali government for control of the country and Al Shabaab, despite losing its foothold in the south of the country, remains a powerful insurgent group responsible for a number of terror attacks in Somalia and Kenya over the last decade. The civil war has continued, with brief periods of respite, for over two decades.

A further contributing factor to widespread displacement of people is the regular occurrence of adverse climate events. In 2011, Somalia suffered a major famine, and a subsequent mass exodus of its people in search of food. A further devastating famine occurred in 2016-17 after a prolonged drought. The UNHCR estimates that more than 810,000 refugees have fled Somalia, (with more than 2.6 million internally displaced persons within the country) (UNHCR 2019). These refugees have scattered mainly throughout neighbouring countries such as Kenya and Ethiopia. Many made their way north by sea across the Gulf of Aden to Yemen. Some refugees have headed for Europe, with the UK hosting a sizeable population, and others have traveled as far afield as Australia. It is worth highlighting that the population of Somalia in the 1970s stood at around 4 million. Even with an increase in population over the past 40 years, the combined total of refugees and asylum seekers as calculated by the UNHCR represents a significant proportion of this population. The population living abroad is crucial in keeping the Somali economy afloat. In 2016, it was estimated that annually 1.4 billion USD is sent to Somalia in the form of remittances, comprising nearly a quarter of the country's GDP (Rift Valley Institute 2018).

◊

There is broad consensus among scholars and the wider public when it comes to significant events in Somalia's recent history as presented in the first part of this chapter. However, overall there is considerable dissent among historians and Somali scholars around a number of issues in Somali history This section looks at some of the more contested issues in the history of Somalia. One factor concerns the availability of documentary evidence. Lewis points out that because the Somali language was not written until 1972, Somalia possesses an 'unusually rich oral literature' (Lewis 2002, 5). Due to absence of written material, there is scant documented evidence available for examining Somali history pre-19th century. However, Somalia has a long history ripe for historical scholarship, and it is crucial to consider this history to produce rounded historical narratives (Weinstein 2005; E. Said 1978; Bayly 1999). This is a challenging project, due to the limited availability of descriptions of Somalia pre 1800. What is available are accounts from early Islamic and Portuguese travellers which concern the coastal towns. 'For the interior, we must rely primarily on oral traditions and narratives' (Besteman 1999, 49).

One early account was that of the explorer Ibn Battuta who arrived in the 14th century to coastal towns producing raw materials and cloth and was amazed to find sophisticated port cities. Other early documented history concerns the arrival of slaves in Somalia from the 17th century onwards who were acquired for work in the textile industry and for agricultural labour.

Being Muslims, Somalis were safe from being enslaved themselves as there is a religious tenet that free Muslims may not be enslaved (Besteman 1999, 51). However, slavery of other groups would continue well into the 20th century, despite the fact that the Italian colonial government issued three ordinances outlawing slavery (Besteman 1999, 55).

◊

The history of commercial and intellectual contact between the inhabitants of the Arabian and Somali coasts may help explain the Somalis' close connection with the Prophet Muhammad (Chapin Metz 1992, 2). The Somali clans claim descent (though distant and mythical) from noble Arab ancestors, even including the prophet Muhammad (Barrows 2008).

Despite the much earlier Muslim settlement in Somalia, large-scale conversion of the Somalis arguably did not take place until the 11th, century with the arrival of powerful Muslim patriarchs, in particular the renowned Sheikh Daarood Jabarti and Sheikh Isaaq. Darood was married to Doombira Dir, the daughter of a local patriarch. This union gave rise to the alliance that forms the largest clan-family in Somalia, the Daarood. Sheikh Isaaq founded the large Isaaq clan-family in northern Somalia (Chapin Metz 1992, 5). Chapin Metz asserts that in addition to the clan system of lineages, the Arabian sheikhs introduced the patriarchal ethos and patrilineal genealogy typical of Semitic societies into Somalia (Chapin Metz 1992, 6). As a result, Islam is inextricably linked to genealogy in Somalia.

Islam is often characterised by mutual dependence between faith and the state (Gellner 1993; An-Na'im 2010). In the case of Somalia, where an already powerful kinship organisation structure existed, Islam was made compatible with the existing social structure. Somalis have maintained their distinct kinship groups, even within the unifying force of Islam. Lewis points out that Islam in Somalia has long been associated with the expression of 'the Sufi, or mystical view of the Muslim faith'. Sufism is more readily accepted in some Muslim countries than others, (it is decried as heresy by the Saudi Arabian Wahhabis (Sedgwick 1997)). It emphasises a personal relationship with God while also exalting 'the charismatic powers of saints'. Thus, it is 'particularly well adapted to the Somali clan system in which clan ancestors readily become transposed into Muslim saints' (Lewis 2002, 64). It is in this way that Islam in Somalia and the clan system are intricately connected and have influenced each other for centuries.

Somalis have modified Islam to fit their particular social and physical environment (for example, merging Islam with the clan system as described). Other modifications include the continued practice of folk or animist religious rituals in treating certain types of illness (including tuberculosis and pneumonia) attributed to spirit possession by folk religion practitioners and believers. Elements of traditional knowledge were also used in astronomical interpretations, marking seasonal changes and times for migration (Chapin Metz 1992, 101-102) and to set the dates of rituals which are specifically Somali. Some Somalis still actively engage in pre-Islamic rituals including a collective rain-making ritual practised in the south.

The vast majority of Somalis today are Sunni Muslims (Sufism is still practised within the broader context of Sunni Islam). Many scholars believe that Islam is a distinguishing factor of great importance for the Somali (Abdullahi 2001; Besteman 1999; Lewis 2002). It has been invoked to explain a supposed sense of singularity among Somalis. Certainly, Somalia is unusual among its neighbours, most of whom are Christians or followers of indigenous African faiths.

◊

In 1961, Ian Lewis described Somali society as consisting of six patrilineal clan-families formed by the descendants of mythical Arabic ancestors who arrived in Somalia 25-35 generations ago. Each clan-family encompassed a set of patrilineally related clans, subclans, sub subclans and lineages (Lewis 1961). Since Lewis' seminal account of Somali pastoral society, much attention has been focussed on the segmentary lineage, the pastoral lifestyle and the strength of Islam in Somalia (Cassanelli 1982; Hassig 1997; Lewis 2002; Samatar 1988). According to Lewis, kinship pervades all aspects of Somali life: personal, political, cultural and religious. The clans can be considered the fundamental political unit in Somalia.

The six Somali clan-families have been likened to the 'Old Testament version of the tribal segmentation of the children of Israel' (Touval 1963, 77).

The pastoral nomadic clan-families comprise the Dir, Isaaq, Hawiye and Darood. The Dir are concentrated in the West, the Isaaq in the central northern and eastern regions and the Darood can be found further east. The Hawiye live mainly in the south. These clans are nomadic and traditionally spend much of the year in transit, while remaining within their broader area of land. The agricultural clan-families comprise the Digil and Rahanwayn. These clans reside in the South of Somalia. In 1961 Lewis estimated that approximately one eighth of the total Somali population were sedentary cultivators (although there has been rapid urbanisation in Somalia since independence). This indicates that the clan system is not purely a locality or class-based system. While the pastoral nomads do move around, they are based within certain regions and move between known points. The agricultural clans are not accorded the same status as the nomadic clans; this may be a result of many agricultural labourers arriving as slaves from the 17th century.

Muhammad Farah Aidid, the de-facto leader of Somalia from 1991 to 1993, describes clans in this way: 'The very fact that this social structure has been continuing for thousands of years without much change despite colonial rule and an oppressive military regime under Siyad Barre shows its strength, utility, and capability to solve the various problems and exigencies of their difficult life' (Aidid and Ruhela 1994, 181). Indeed, other scholars have pointed out how uniquely suited the clan system is to the particular challenges and requirements of living in Somalia. Ken Menkhaus explains that 'the law and order Somalia enjoyed prior to the 1980s — and Somalia was unquestionably one of the safest places in Africa — was a reflection of the social contract more than the capacity of the police (or of a central government)' (Menkhaus 2004, 32-33). The flexible reciprocity network formed by the clans, and the social security provided by this indigenous governance is not bound to a centralised structure in the way many modern governance systems are.

However, kinship has also divided Somalia. The clan system has existed in Somalia for much longer than any form of centralised government, and the two governance systems have not co-existed peacefully. Siyad Barre's nationalist campaign of the late 1970s intended to abolish divisions based on social inequality (Besteman 1999, 113). The campaign aimed to draw the clans together under one national flag. In this quest for unification, tribalism was condemned as the most serious impediment to national unity. Barre denounced it as a 'disease' obstructing development not only in Somalia, but also throughout the developing world. Harsh punishments were meted out to those engaging in activities that amounted to tribalism (Chapin Metz 1992).

Survival in a context of environmental scarcity requires cooperation and strong networks, however it is limiting to consider the clans only as a response to environmental hardship. It also risks politicising robust and functional social security networks, and reducing the clans to units, which exist in a state of perpetual mutual opposition. This can be glimpsed in an early statement from Lewis: 'In the harsh struggle for survival which is a nomad's lot, suspicion is the natural attitude towards those with whom one competes for access to scarce pasture and water. This defence mechanism is extended to all contexts of social interaction and hence becomes a national characteristic' (Hesse 2010, 250). Despite this dated explanation of the way individuals are pitted against each other in a struggle for survival, the clan system has been able to maintain a fragmented stability across the country, based on decentralised indigenous governance systems.

◊

Social stratification derived from ethnicity based on the unique Somali-Muslim heritage is an import factor in Somali life. As outlined above, Somali life was organised through the governance framework of the clans for centuries. The clans are said to originate with a single male ancestor, the mythical founding father, 'Samaale' or 'Samaal' (Chapin Metz 1992, 71). This seems to be intimately linked with Somali-Muslim heritage, and the literature points to those Somalis with lighter skin (i.e. the descendents of the Arab Samaal) considering themselves superior to their darker skinned counterparts. Social inequality in Somalia is associated with lineage and clan affiliation and determined partly by physical appearance (Chapin Metz 1992, 78). Besteman points out that despite the existence of laws prohibiting the use of terms to distinguish ethnic groups, the Gosha of Southern Somalia are labelled by many such terms (including *boon* – person of low status, *addoon* – slave and *jareer* – rough hair texture). Jareer denotes those who are of 'African' and thus slave ancestry as opposed to the mythical Arabic ancestry of Somalis (Besteman 1999, 115-116). While Lewis argues that the distinction between slaves and the noble classes is clear in northern Somalia (Lewis 1955, 125), according to Besteman in the south, the distinctions have become blurred due to a wider variety of commoner groups (Besteman 1999, 123).

Some texts refer to the two mainly agriculturist clans of Digil and Rahanwayn using the derogatory term Saab (ignoble) (Chapin Metz 1992, 77). Saab is a term signifying those who pursue certain low-status occupations. The Samaal felt that the Saab had lowered themselves by their reliance on agriculture and their willingness to absorb foreigners into their clan in what has been described as 'borderline xenophobia' (Hesse 2010, 249). Certainly, it is arguable that southern Somalis suffered more than their fellow citizens, both at the hands of colonisers, and then at the hands of their own government: The southern (agricultural) Somalis residing in the valleys of the Juba and Shabeele rivers had their lands seized and taken over by colonial plantations, while they themselves were forced to work for colonial labour schemes. They then lost their rights to their land through Barre's socialist nationalisation laws and suffered terribly through the Cold War militarisation of Somalia. During the civil war, the southern lands especially were sites of massacres, and in the more recent famines of the 2000s, the southerners again suffered disproportionately compared to their northern counterparts (McMichael 2003).

These differences in social standing highlight both the absence of Somali homogeneity and the social stratification that is so significant to Somali history. Some attribute this stratification directly to the clan system. According to Besteman, the social organisation of Somali society lends itself to conceptions of inferiority through the 'investment of notions of lineal purity in the clan structure' (Besteman 1999, 123). While Somali clans are fiercely egalitarian with regard to leadership and political control, they contain divisions of unequal status. The primary division between those of lower castes and the 'pure blooded' clan members is that the lower castes are not able to claim direct lineal descent from the clan's founding ancestor.

The nomadic castes trace their line back to a common mythical level of ancestry, and members of a clan family can often trace their genealogy back some thirty generations to a common ancestor (Lewis 1994, 20). However the presence of significant minority groups, such as Somalis with Arab-Persian or slavery heritage (Besteman 1999) is both a challenge to the segmentary lineage model and evidence of the widespread social stratification within Somalia.

◊

The regime of Siyad Barre is generally reviled among Somalis today, and there is no doubt that he was largely responsible for the civil war and the ensuing conflict and chaos. However, it was a period of immense social and cultural change in Somalia and as such, deserves closer attention. When Barre came to power in 1969, he set out to change the fabric of Somali society radically. Socialism was gaining traction in Africa in the phase of de-colonisation and Barre employed his own particular version of 'Scientific Socialism' in order to achieve his vision. This severely curtailed the operation of the clan system and in fact was a transition to anti-tribalism altogether. Barre aimed to achieve a sense of national unity and a Pan-Somalism (Lewis 2002, 209).

There was considerable conflict between the government's desire to modernise and unify the country and the pre-existing way of life. In order to eradicate traditional clan activities, Barre forbade such activities as *diya* (blood compensation) and introduced a state-controlled death penalty instead. Another initiative to curb the rural clan dependence saw the government provide money for funeral expenses of those that died in towns with no family members. There was also a state sponsored program to urbanise the country and relocate nomads. Even the traditional greeting of *ina adeer* (cousin) was replaced by *jaalle* (friend, comrade) to minimise connotations of kinship (Lewis 1994, 150-155).

Barre also introduced positive change during his leadership. One of the clearest examples is his push to create a national written language. Up to this point, there had been no indigenous written language and because colonial activities had required northern Somalis to use English and the southern Somalis to use Italian, there were serious communication issues within the country. Illiteracy rates were very high, so the task was daunting. The government created a written language using the Roman alphabet and instigated an intensive literacy campaign. Following a year of teaching in urban areas, more than 30,000 students were sent into the country to teach the nomadic Somalis (Moore 2007, 13). This had a positive effect on the pan-national sentiment of Somalis and increased efficiency of the civil services. The literacy rate also reached 60% by the late 1970s (Samatar 1988, 103).

In addition to the campaign to eradicate illiteracy, Barre adopted educational policies which focussed on an expanded and accessible technical education system and the development of higher education options in Somalia. Tertiary-level courses available in the capital Mogadishu included law, teaching, agriculture, economics, engineering, and medicine. By the early 1980s, considerable progress had been made towards Barre's ambitious educational goals. All schools were nationalised and there were four levels of education. However, the progress was not uniform. Many girls and children from nomadic groups only completed half of the eight-year primary curriculum and enrolments beyond primary school continued to be low even in the late 1980s. Likewise, the education reforms were not as successful in reaching the rural population, where despite enormous efforts on the part of the government to restructure the school system to encourage further study, high levels of secondary and technical school drop-out rates persisted (Keating and Simons 2008, 3).

The collapse of the Somali state and the subsequent civil war altered Somali life irrevocably. This was particularly devastating in the area of education. The education system in Somalia broke down entirely between 1987 and 1991 (Keating and Simons 2008, 1). Many adult Somalis had access to a reasonable level of education, promoted by a culture of pride surrounding education, with a select class of older Somalis also being able to access British and Italian schools. However, anyone born in the 1970s or 1980s in Somalia had a partial or disrupted education at best, with a complete halt to schooling post 1991. This has created a generational divide, with some older Somalis possessing a much higher level of education than their children and even grandchildren.

◊

Scholarship on the formation and expression of national identity focusses on the sharing of social experience amongst a defined community. Emphasis is placed on common language, education, and uniting under one banner in conflict. Key here is the shared social experience: celebrating the same victories and mourning the same losses in a common language create a feeling of common identity.

Despite the relative ethnic and religious homogeneity in Somalia, it is hard to overstate the challenges to Somali national unity. Commentators often highlight the fragmented nature of the social and cultural landscape, despite ethnic and religious homogeneity. As with many African nations which were carved up in the 1880s by invading colonial powers, the borders on the map do not correlate with indigenous alliances and distributions. In fact, the Somali flag has a star with five points, which represent the territories where there has traditionally been a concentration of Somali peoples. These include the British and Italian Somalilands (now the Somalia of most maps). The other three points stand for Djibouti, the northeast corner of Kenya, and the contested Ogaden region in Ethiopia.

In the words of Hyndman: 'The imagined pan-Somali nation has never corresponded to the colonial nor post-colonial borders of the country' (Hyndman 1999, 159). The rift between colonial and ethnic borders has resulted in conflict and violence, especially in Kenya where there is a large population of ethnic Somalis. Tension between the Kenyan government and this population is high, and surveillance and expulsion of Somalis by the Kenyan government was common. Al Shabaab has responded violently in Kenya in retaliation.

Somali efforts to form a nation state have been hampered by the legacy of the European partition of Africa, the empire building activities of Ethiopia and the segmentation resulting from Somali clanship (Barrows 2008). Territorially, at least, Somalia has long been a contested concept, even among Somalis (Hesse 2010). The disputed ownership of the Ogaden valley in Ethiopia, (where many ethnic Somalis reside) has been a source of conflict within Somalia and between Somalia and neighbouring countries for centuries.

As described, the Somali prize their Arabian connections and value those traditions which proclaim their descent from noble Arabian lineages and from the family of the Prophet (Lewis 2002, 5). The Somali language is also clear evidence of this contact, containing a considerable number of Arabic loan-words. Arabic itself is sufficiently widely known to be regarded almost as a second language.

Besteman argues that ex-slaves arriving in Somalia 'adopted clan affiliations as an aspect of personal identity, to negotiate social relations, and to build kinship networks' (Besteman 1999, 113). She claims that by the 1970s, mid Gosha valley villagers (largely comprised of descendants of slaves) spoke only Somali dialects, practiced Islam and shared Somali cultural values. This 'Somalization' of slave descendants gave the impression that Somalia was linguistically, culturally and religiously united (Besteman 1999, 114). It also problematises the popular conception of clans as ancient bloodlines and highlights the flexibility of this social construct.

◊

It is imperative to consider the multi-faceted dimensions that influence the social, political and religious domains in modern Somalia.

These are heavily rooted in the pre- and post-colonial events, and the gap between what is accepted history, and what is contested history deserves further attention.

Indigenous governance remains an operational and dynamic system, despite steps towards centralised government over the last decade. The indigenous governance systems are symbolic of the complex, moveable and flexible systems that endure within Somalia. These systems are highly evolved and rely on cooperation from all invested members. A further example of this mutual trust in Somalia is the informal *hawala* network, which supports money transfers, both within Somalia, and externally. Hawala is based on trust relationships and allows the transfer of money where neither the sender nor receiver has a bank account (LSE 2019). The system is well suited to Somalia, particularly in the absence of central financial systems. The reciprocity networks discussed are based on equal investment by all members in order to function fully and well. This underscores the notion that reciprocity is extremely important to achieve public stability, which is particularly pertinent at a time where there is mistrust of the central government among the Somali people. They suffered at the hands of their government before and during the civil war and citizens have endured repression and violence from the centralised government in more recent years.

Clans are a dominant topic in the current academic discourse around Somalia, with much attention devoted to broad questions concerning belonging and identity. Limited attention has been focussed on the unique and effective cultural social control mechanisms that have been disrupted over the last 200 years. There is room for more academic exploration of the operational mechanisms of indigenous government, and how these might be harnessed to improve social cohesion in conjunction with the newly developing centralised government. It is difficult to view Somalia through a traditional neoliberal lens, where following state collapse and failure, a centralised democratic government restores peace and stability. This lens does not take into account the many factors that make Somalia an unusual and unique case and ignores the exisiting indigenous structures which have worked so well for so long.

Post-independence, many scholars assumed that Somalia would be a promising case for state-making in the Sub-Saharan African context. This optimism was perhaps due to a perceived cultural, linguistic and religious homogeneity in Somalia. Setting aside the trauma of colonisation and the decades of ineffective communication due to the use of English and Italian by the respective Northern and Southern colonial governments, other factors have hindered the creation of a strong Somali state. The contested borders, coupled with strong social stratification, and the presence of the clans as social control mechanisms do not lend themselves to nation building in the neoliberal sense.

Somalia is complex. Elements that seem clear are in fact often quite opaque. For example, Islam is undoubtedly a strong force in Somalia. However, as shown, it has been adapted to suit tribal religions that predate Islam's arrival in Somalia. It also includes elements that are specific to the geographic and cultural context of Somalia.

Similarly, while the native language is shared across the nation, it was not written down until 1972. Accordingly, Somalia boasts a strong oral culture. Poetry is prized and is a living and dynamic link with the history of the area and the Somali people. This oral history is rich and elegant, with emphasis on style and skill in poetry and story-telling. However, this means historical accounts were written only by foreign authors. This reliance on external sources for written history reduces the strength of indigenous voices in actively telling their story and interpreting and reinterpreting their history. It also means that Somalia does not have a strong, consistent historical narrative that can be engaged with by outsiders.

This poses numerous problems. Firstly, because in times of political upheaval and conflict, there are attempts to create and promulgate certain narratives that benefit powerful actors. Given the lack of written history of the region, it is difficult to find source material to counter such narratives. With increased interest in the area due to the focus on terrorism and the consideration of Somalia as a failed state, there are additional perspectives that are being disseminated widely in the media and political circles. These narratives also do not come from within Somalia, but are the product of external powers, with vested interests and agendas.

This also leads to a consistent portrayal of Somalia as a place of conflict and anarchy which fails to acknowledge the highly evolved and complex social control mechanisms that have maintained the social contract with some success despite the colonial invasion. Scholars would do well to provide a counterbalance – a complex and more nuanced take on Somali history.

◊

Somalis constitute one of the largest African refugee populations currently living in Australia. In 2006 the Census recorded 4,314 Somalis living in Australia. In 2011 that number increased by a third. The census in 2016, recorded 7,668 Somali born people living in Australia. Somalis first started arriving in Australia in the late 1980s when the regime in Somalia began to oppress and attack its opposition in the North. This displacement accelerated after the total collapse of the Barre government in 1991 and the beginning of the civil war (Ramsden and Ridge 2012, 227). During this chaotic period, food scarcity due to the drought and the political upheaval prompted many more Somalis to leave the country. This movement continued well into the 2000s (Gundel 2002, 241).

Around half of these newly arrived Somalis settled in Victoria, and many have made the inner north and western suburbs of Melbourne home. Many of the Somalis that have immigrated to Australia are from urban backgrounds; most from the capital, Mogadishu (Ramsden and Ridge 2012, 227). The vast majority of Somali migrants in Melbourne arrived as refugees under the humanitarian program and because of the civil war, many Somalis have lived in other countries en route to Australia (Clyne and Kipp 1999, 4-5), often in refugee camps with very limited access to education facilities so for many younger people, their first exposure to any system of education was in Australia, often at a relatively advanced age (up to ten or eleven years old).

Census data indicate that Somalis in Melbourne reside around four main areas. These are Heidelberg West greater area, the North Melbourne/Flemington greater area, the inner North East (Carlton, Collingwood and Fitzroy), and the inner West, most notably, Braybrook. The Heidelberg West and the North Melbourne/Flemington areas are hubs of community activity: In Heidelberg West alone, 9.39% of the suburb population speaks Somali. As a proportion of all who speak Somali in Melbourne, if the surrounding suburbs are included as well, the Heidelberg West and North Melbourne/Flemington areas account for over 40% of this group.

In the Heidelberg West wider area, 50.0% of people with Somali ancestry were born in Somalia, and 17.3% were born in a location other than Australia (presumably in transit to Australia). In the North Melbourne/Flemington area, these figures are 46.6% born in Somalia and 15.8% born outside Australia. These figures indicated the presence of Gen 1.5 Somali Australians in these suburbs.

The age of people this research engaged with ranged from the 60s to late teens and early 20s; that is they were born between 1949 and 1996. The oldest people in their 60s are still playing a relatively active part in cultural life, participating in cultural events, festivals and community meetings. All of the young people had finished high school, and many were studying at tertiary level.

The Somali family size was significantly larger than the Australian norm. The most common number of children per couple in Australia is two (Australian Bureau of Statistics 2016), while for the Somali families in this study, it was five. In general, the older people had the largest families, and the younger people had smaller families. Family size was defined as immediate family — if someone had children, this included their partner and their children; if they did not have children, then this figure included their siblings and parents. This was an important distinction, as it is culturally normal for Somalis to think of families as extended family groups. Similarly, the term 'household size' was not used to avoid confusion by including relatives who were staying for a short period (perhaps between jobs, between houses, or settling into a new area).

Interestingly, none of the respondents lived alone, or with friends or colleagues in a share-house situation. They were either living at home with their parents, or they had moved out with a spouse and had children of their own. The smallest family size was four, with only three instances of this. These were young Somali-born people who had moved out of their parents' home with a spouse and had two children.

The educational attainment of the people in this study varied widely, according to age. The majority of the respondents who had only primary school education were aged above 50. A likely explanation is that when these people were of primary school age, the education system in Somalia had not yet been modernised. This was also a time when Somalia was still much less urbanised, thus it is likely that at least some of these people lived rurally at a significant distance from high schools, and so were not able to attend. The generation of people who were able to attend school between 1960-

1980 had high rates of attainment, in line with the rapidly developing education system in Somalia. Those who attended school after the 1980s had lower attainment, which is most likely because the increasingly desperate situation in Somalia under Barre's regime caused the shutdown of the educational system.

This shows that the Somali Australian community has a variety of needs, based on their age and qualifications. This complex picture of uneven educational attainment means that the community has significant challenges to meet in terms of participating fully in Australian life. The following section looks to some of the challenges that all refugees face, and then focusses on the difficulties that are particular to the Somali community in Melbourne.

◊

There is no doubt that Muslim migrants and refugees settling in Australia have encountered particular challenges. The disruptions to their lives were likely compounded upon arrival in Australia, with its different cultural, language and social norms (Pittaway and Muli 2009, 31).

There are many structural constraints and conditions confronting migrants and refugees in their new environment that shape the kinds of family arrangements, roles, and orientations that emerge among them. So do the norms and values they encounter in their new homes. On the other hand, migrants and refugees are not passive individuals who are merely acted upon by external forces. They play an active role in reconstructing and redefining family life. Indeed, members of the family, by virtue of their gender and generation, have differing interests so that women (and men) and young people (and older people) often try to fashion family patterns in ways that improve their positions and further their aims (Kibria 1993; Oxfeld 1993; Foner 1997).

The displacement of Somalis has affected their ethnic, cultural and religious practices in their host countries for a number of reasons. One example is the way that sex and age ratios affect family patterns in the composition of migrant groups. Speaking about migrant families more generally, Foner notes that if men greatly outnumber women, this can lead to women having more power in relationships (Foner 1997). Large numbers of older people can also affect family dynamics as they may watch children while parents are working. They may also provide the strongest representation of pre-migration beliefs and practices within families. When older individuals are absent from a community, men may be forced to take a more active role in household responsibilities because there are fewer adults within households (Foner 1997, 964).

Migrants are also exposed to different customs, religions, and political ideals. This is apparent in many areas, perhaps most strongly in male-female relations and the question of gender roles and the relationship between younger generations and their parents and grandparents. Women are generally much more enthusiastic than men to endorse values that enhance women's position and young people also generally enjoy their new freedoms, which their parents may resist (Foner 1997, 971). Furthermore, government assistance, if provided, can allow individuals to be more independent. In general, earnings and entitlements translate into greater autonomy and power. Perhaps unsurprisingly, women are often more receptive to notions of gender equality than men (Foner 1997). There is strong evidence of this in the Somali community in Melbourne, however it is wrong to assume that women are perceived as inferior, or less powerful than men in Somalia, as will be discussed in further detail in chapter 6.

There is some indication that the majority of Somalis in Melbourne have come from large towns or cities in Somalia, which would suggest that adult Somalis arriving in Victoria during the first wave of refugee intake were urban, and most likely to have benefited from Barre's educational policies and programs (A. Said 2005). At the 2001 Census, nearly half of Victoria's Somali population was under 25 years old. This means that half the Somali population living in Victoria in 2001 was part of the generation of Somalis who were under the age of 14 in 1990, when the school system ceased to exist. The remaining half fell either into the category of Somalis who had the opportunity under the Barre regime to access a university-level education, or who were over 35 and may have received an education in the British or Italian education system (Keating and Simons 2008).

Somali culture is strongly oriented to spoken language. Until the 1970s, northern Somali education was conducted in English and Latin script became the official script of the Somali language. This means that in Somalia, anyone born prior to 1950 had very little chance of becoming literate in their own language, and achieving literacy in another language would also have been extremely difficult. Nevertheless, there were some educated Somalis who did speak and write English and Italian, as the Italian and British colonial authorities had established a schooling system and set their own curriculum. This was, however, only available to a very select minority, who often trained as interpreters, and worked mainly as administrative assistants. There would also have been merchants who were able to communicate in different languages (Arabic, Swahili for example) as the ports in the Gulf of Aden were commercial hubs. However, documentary evidence is difficult to find due to the tendency of historical accounts to define education in terms of a narrow scope (Miller 2004). There is a propensity in educational histories to ignore (or forget) educational experiences outside this scope, such as female experiences, experiences of the poor and experiences of educational enrichment outside the context of mass schooling.

Only a small portion of the total population would have had access to these educational experiences. Thus, the majority of Somalis born before 1960 arriving in Australia would not have had access to education beyond primary school level. Many of the young people spoke about their grandparents' limited educational attainments and the way they pressured their children and grandchildren to obtain a good education, as they had been unable to.

Somalis (particularly the urban dwellers who migrated to Australia) value education highly, and aspirations to attain a university education and a professional career are high among the community in Australia. However, there is a lack of understanding within the older Somali generation of the breadth of education and training options available in Australia. This can lead to conflict between parents and children whose educational choices the parents do not endorse. For example, young Somali Australians choosing to enter a vocational study pathway often struggle to communicate to their families that their choices are reasonable, as apprenticeships are generally not highly valued within the community (Keating and Simons 2008, 3).

The value of education is a key Somali cultural concept: Education is also highly esteemed among Somali youth in America and has been described as the most valued piece of cultural capital for the Somali youth. This is because education allows Somalis living abroad to fulfill the 'cultural expectation to financially help family members in the United States or still in Somalia, Ethiopia, or Kenya' (Bigelow 2010, 149).

The importance the Somali community places on education is remarkable. The young people described the expectations their parents have of them, and their sometimes unrealistic hopes about their children's future professions. Many young men especially explained that the previous generation had little understanding of the scope of the VET system in Australia and also saw little value in practical training such as apprenticeships. The young people all agreed that there were a select group of professions which were most favoured (perhaps predictably, medical and legal were often mentioned), and that there were other professions which were disappointing to Somali parents.

All of the young women I met with were either working or studying with the idea of gaining employment later. Some ridiculed the notion that they should stay at home and not work. Although they plan to take a break from working when they have children, they were certain that they would return to work when their children began school. This shift in gender identities has been noted in other African communities in Australia (Hatoss and Huijser 2010, 156).

Another significant issue raised was refugee status. There are millions of globally displaced Somalis, and their experiences as refugees set them apart from voluntary migrants. By definition, the circumstances that lead to a refugee experience disrupt the 'home country' in some way — personal and societal upheavals go hand in hand. For example, refugees often have to overcome unique obstacles to maintain contact with family members left behind or scattered around the globe (Herger Boyle and Ali 2010, 47).

For refugees, sending societies intentionally or unintentionally create barriers to transnational ties, and situational contexts in the sending country will influence refugee transnationalism. If the sending society is in disarray, as is the case in Somalia, formal communication networks are jeopardised. For example, the difficulty of maintaining close ties with family in the sending society may make it easier to reject pre-migration beliefs because there is less informal social control on the refugee (Herger Boyle and Ali 2010, 50). For the Somali community in Melbourne, this was more true for the parents of the respondents, as the young people tended to keep in regular contact with relatives and friends in Somalia via social media.

Somali refugees have commonly fled to neighbouring countries. Camps in Kenya and Ethiopia have provided a temporary haven for the majority of displaced Somalis, but small numbers have also gone to Yemen, Djibouti, Tanzania and Egypt. Some have resettled in European countries and North America, as well as Australia. Many people have lost contact with family and friends in the context of this scattering. Somali immigrants to Australia include a relatively high proportion of women with their children, whose husbands and other male relatives have died or are missing (Williams 2003). These families may be separated from family support and structures they would normally rely on in Somalia. They have also experienced high levels of trauma, deprivation, and distress, and may be suffering the effects of such experiences. There are relatively few older males, who traditionally play a significant role in the development of male adolescents and young men (Hurd, Zimmerman, and Xue 2009). This means that community structures to support cultural maintenance or the negotiation of new values have to be created in Australia at the same time as settlement is occurring. This social upheaval places significant stress on traditional family practices and norms and can leave individuals feeling untethered from their family roles.

It is important to highlight here, as McGown does (1999), that while migrants and refugees are undoubtedly influenced by the host country's values, customs, religion and social norms, this process is dynamic and mutual. Arriving populations also change the host country. It is difficult to imagine what Melbourne would be like today without the coffee culture brought by post-war migrants. However, at the time of arrival the European immigrants bringing these novelties were marginalised and victims of racism due to cultural differences (Burnside 2013). Now, Melbourne is proud of its cafe culture, and the cosmopolitan variety of food available all over the city. When we spoke about the possibility of something similar happening for Somali (and in general, African) refugees, community members were circumspect. They didn't believe that their culture could have such a strong influence in Australia, because of the small numbers of African migrants in Australia and because the differences in culture were just too great.

This supports McGown's thesis that the further apart the receiving and arriving cultures are, the harder it is for them to integrate and become comfortable with each other (1999).The visible difference of Somalis must be considered. Their dark skin, their conservative dress and their religious identity mark them as different immediately. It has been noted that religious identity in particular, can be a barrier to settlement if a refugee feels that their religion is threatened (Moghissi 2006; Yuval-Davis 2006). Indeed, unfavourable reception of this facet of identity can lead to increased religiosity. Moghissi, writing about identity formation in the Muslim diaspora, states: 'In the case of diasporas of Islamic cultures… the formation of a collective identity, or diasporic consciousness and solidarity, is more often a response to an inhospitable climate in the host societies than an expression of cultural nostalgia' (Moghissi 2006, xv). This process can be either positive or negative and this depends on the response of the host society. He gives the example of schools being open and tolerant of religious dress and prayer at school as a means to encouraging greater integration, while an unreceptive and closed society can create a greater religious conservatism 'than that which was actually experienced … in the home country' (Moghissi 2006, xvi).

It may be that political cultures that are more welcoming of ethnic or religious minorities, and allow social participation without disadvantaging them for their ethnic or religious affiliation will ease the process of cultural weaving for immigrants (McGown 1999, 7).

It's also worth remembering that at least some of those people who flee persecution from Muslim majority countries may have been targeted for their liberal views in their home country, and in fact are not usually religiously conservative. However, upon arrival in an unreceptive host country, they adopt a more religious identity as a means of protection and solidarity with others in a similar situation (Wharton 2014). The young people I spoke with explained that their parents held tightly to their religion as marker of identity and that religion had become more important to them in Australia than it was at home in Somalia.

One strategy employed by the Somali community in Melbourne in the face of myriad challenges is based on their strong collective identity, and provides community support in a sometimes hostile environment. On many occasions it was observed that the Somalis seemed to have a distinct sense of self, and a habit of setting themselves apart, both from other minority groups such as other refugees and migrants, and from mainstream Australians. This has been noted by other authors (Hesse 2010; Chapin Metz 1992), and particularly in the Australian context (Ramsden and Taket 2013, 99-100).

This idea was conveyed by many of the young people in mostly positive ways. For example, some members of the older generations prided themselves on their success in Australia, despite their extreme disadvantage at the time of arrival. The younger people often stated that while they had other Muslim friends, there were cultural differences between them, and it was often easier to maintain friendships with other Somalis. The women in particular distinguished the strength and pride of Somali women as something that set them apart.

In North Melbourne, I noted that the older Somali men who congregate at the community centre seemed to keep themselves apart from other community centre users. Observation of the people making use of the facilities showed that these were almost all men in the early afternoon, with patrons comprising a mix of ethnicities including Vietnamese, South American (particularly Chilean and Argentinian) and Horn of Africa groups. I noted that while some of the other men played cards and had discussions in English, the Somalis preferred to speak their own language and keep to themselves. There was no hostility, rather a polite distance between the groups, possibly due to language and communication difficulties, and also because the Somalis are likely to be much more recent arrivals than some other groups who largely arrived in Australia in the 1970s.

A different explanation was offered by an experienced social worker in the area who explained that while other migrant groups established connections within their own ethnic community first, and then branched out and began to interact with other groups, the Somalis she had worked with had been less likely to seek connections with non-Somalis. She argued that they were remarkably self-contained and did not see a need or benefit to expanding their relationships beyond their immediate circle. This idea was reinforced by one of my own experiences during a visit to a group of older women at a home in an apartment building in North Melbourne, inhabited by people of diverse ethnicities. For this reason the building had been selected as a site for improvement through increased social interaction between residents. To this end, a social organisation had set up some regular events. These were intended to be relaxed, with a variety of food and some planned activities. The activities were designed to keep the residents coming back to the next event.

For example, one week there was a photo station and the residents were invited to have their photo taken. They would need to return the following week to collect them and take part in the next stage of the activities. According to the organising social workers, these parties were well attended by the residents, however, Somalis were notably underrepresented. On the occasion of my visit, one of these events was in full swing in the congregation area downstairs, and outside in the playground. However, there was a party in full swing in the flat I was visiting as well. There was music, there was food, and flat held approximately 12 women aged between 40 and 65 who were enjoying themselves very much, albeit far away from the planned event downstairs. When asked why they were not attending the other event their response was dismissive. One of the women replied 'Why would we, when everything we need is here?' Others said that they felt more comfortable among their friends and family and therefore did not wish to attend. They seemed puzzled by the concept of the events, designed to bring together residents from different backgrounds and situations. The general feeling was that this was not necessary as they had their own groups already.

This particular strategy relies on strong community links and a sense of reciprocity which is similar to the strong social contractr in Somalia. It has manifested in many different ways, sometimes to the advantage of the community, particularly where they have robust support networks. However, sometimes it has caused individuals to shun other forms of outside assistance, which might have been better able to meet particular needs. The following section moves from examining community identity and expression to more theoretical notions of how individual identity is conceived and sustained.

3

The framing of Somali identities

Theories of identity have traced an interesting trajectory over the centuries — from the pre-enlightenment notion that identity was conferred by external (moral) authorities, to the post-enlightenment idea that the identity was more personal and internal, and finally to the commonly accepted idea today that identity is, in many senses, socially constructed (Riley 2007; C. Taylor 1989; Rorty 1976).

John Hewitt has elaborated a tri-partite definition of identity comprising of: situational identity, social identity, and personal identity (Hewitt 2003, 98-113). Situational identities are those which are predominant in face-to-face interactions with others. This concept is certainly not a new one and was described as early as 1937 by William Isaac Thomas. Thomas wrote that upon entering the presence of others, we mutually construct a definition of the situation (Thomas 1937). The ability to define our own and others' *situational identities* enables us to know how to act (and not to act). It also informs our expectations and interpretations of behaviour, both our own, and others' (Vryan, Adler, and Adler 2003, 368). We reveal our situational identities in various ways, especially through language and appearance. This allows those we are interacting with to define or place us in the given social situation (Stone 1962, 92). Situational identities are necessarily in a state of constant flux, and are able to change rapidly in dynamic, interactive environments. However, according to Hewitt, some aspects of identity are more stable and enduring (Hewitt 1989). Our appearance and ethnic identification are clear examples of this.

As we move across situational identities, we define *social identities* for ourselves and others based on group memberships. These social identities remain relatively stable across different situational contexts. The membership groups are most often derived from ascribed characteristics and socially constructed categories such as gender, ethnicity, age, religion, and class. While they provide meanings and labels that define who we are, they depend upon mutual recognition by ourselves and at least some others (Burke 2003).

Personal identity describes the efforts of an individual to construct and preserve an 'autobiography' or 'life story', which helps establish a sense of difference from others (Hewitt 2003). Erving Goffman explains that personal identity involves distinctive traits of individuals, including their name and appearance, personal history and information, personality characteristics, and their special place in a particular kinship network (Goffman 1963). Jan Stets goes a step further and demarcates personal identity as the identity that defines us as unique individuals (Stets 1995). While the distinctions between situational, social, and personal identity are a useful conceptual tool, there is no suggestion that these forms of identity are mutually exclusive. In any given exchange or relationship, all three or any combination of these identities is relevant to the thinking and behavior of participants (Vryan, Adler, and Adler 2003).

In a particularly influential formulation, Stuart Hall argues that we should not discuss one identity, but rather focus on *identities* because in his view, there are 'processes that constitute and continuously re-form the subject'. Identities can therefore be understood as 'temporary attachments', which allow for the continual re-articulation of the self. Hall describes identities as 'narratives': the 'stories we tell about ourselves' (Hall 1995, 65-66). These are contingent on location (especially pertinent for migrants and refugees) and context and this contextuality leads Hall to describe identities as 'sliding'. (Hall 1995, 65-66)For Hall, identities are attached to more than one particular marker or classification (religious, ethnic, national, etc.) (Hall 1995, 66).

In discussing the construction of Muslim identities in Mali, Louis Brenner describes identity as 'a process of naming: naming of self, naming of others, naming *by* others' (Brenner 1993, 59). In his work there is a consistent emphasis on the nature of identity as 'constructed and reconstructed by self and/or others through continuing actions and discourse in a political context' (Brenner 1993, 59). Brenner describes action and discourse as religiously inspired and also as motivated by social, political and economic systems and incentives (Brenner 1993, 59). Thus, the process of 'naming' of both individuals and groups takes place against the background of the broader socio-economic context. Given the influencing factors on the construction and formation of identity, the investigation of the dynamics behind the labels people give to themselves and each other is able to provide insight into processes of social transformation. One major limit to Brenner's notion of identity as 'naming' (which he uses chiefly due to pragmatic considerations) is that it does not account for the many complexities that comprise the issue of identity and identification, rather it presents the notion of 'labelling' as a working definition of the concept of identity.

Yuval-Davis discusses the establishment of cultural identities by refugees in their adopted homelands, and the various influences that affect this in great detail. She describes how factors such as gender, ethnicity, class and the very fact of being a refugee are used as markers to identify where an individual stands in terms of the 'grids of power relations in society' (Yuval-Davis 2006, 199).

Like Hall, she highlights the importance of the 'stories people tell themselves and others about who they are (and who they are not)' (Yuval-Davis 2006, 200). She believes that it is possible to force constructions of self and identity on people (Yuval-Davis 2006, 202).

Numerous investigations of the role of religion in maintaining group identity and solidarity have been conducted, particularly in the case of migrants and refugees living in diaspora (Herberg 1955; Haddad and Lummis 1987; Gibson 1988; Hammond 1988; Warner and Wittner 1998; Ebaugh and Chafetz 2000; Min and Kim 2002). Many of these studies examine the nexus between religion and ethnic identity. Additionally, many scholars have acknowledged and documented the enduring importance of religion in the preservation of cultural and ethnic traditions (Althoff 2006; Hammond 1988). Religion is understood to support the adjustment of first generation immigrants to a new host society, and provide a source of identity (although, often highly contested) for the second generation.

Different migrant groups, undoubtedly, conceive of and integrate their religious and ethnic identities in distinctive ways (Williams 1988, 12-13). Some communities emphasise religious identity more than their ethnic foundation, whereas others focus on ethnic identity and rely on religious institutions to preserve cultural traditions and ethnic boundaries (Yang and Ebaugh 2001, 367).

Immigration itself has at times been described as a theologizing experience, as migrants and refugees are faced with stress, alienation, and confusion that result from their arrival in a new country, which in turn encourages an increased religiosity (Smith 1978, 1175). Thus, we can see the building of religious institutions and the establishment of familiar social and cultural activities within them as an attempt to resolve adjustment issues in the new host society (Rayaprol 1997; Kurien 1998). This can lead to a situation where religion assumes greater importance in the receiving country than it had before arrival.

Religion can also be used as a marker of personal and social distinctiveness in a multicultural context (Rayaprol 1997; Kurien 1998). As strong religious orientation is becoming less common in pluralistic and secular societies, members of a particular faith group may become more conscious of their traditions and transmit their beliefs, values, and behaviours more resolutely (Warner 1998, 17). Religious dress (particularly pertinent in the case of Islam), practices, and organisational affiliations serve as identity markers that help to promote individual self-awareness and preserve group cohesion (R.B. Williams 1988). This is how religious, ethnic, and national heritage is displayed and thus maintained (Kurien 1998).

In this way, religious expression may in fact ease the tensions between refugees and mainstream society by acting as a clearly understood identity 'marker' (Feher 1998; Yang 1999). It is possible that ethnic variation becomes less problematic when individuals define themselves first and foremost in religious terms. This may enable diverse communities to be brought together through shared worship (Sullivan 2000; Feher 1998; Yang 1999). Membership in some kind of religious organisation has also been shown to have psychological and social benefits. These include: economic opportunities, connection to community networks, access to educational resources and a sense of peer trust and support (Hurh and Kim 199; C. Chen 2002). These benefits all reduce social isolation for migrants and refugees (Kwon 2000). One can posit that as these benefits increase, individuals will be more likely to affiliate religiously.

◊

The formation, expression and representation of identity are intricately connected to notions of power. Understanding various forms of power and its manifestations is central to understanding the forces that inform Gen 1.5 Somali identity. There is a large volume of literature on the notion of power, and its connection with identity construction (Barton and Tusting 2005; Clarke 2008). For many years now, the social sciences have looked to the work of Michel Foucault, whilst drawing on earlier influences (such as Friedrich Nietzsche), and later additions (such as to Slavoj Žižek) to Foucault's work. Power is intricately connected with human activity. In Foucault's words 'Power is everywhere; not because it embraces everything, but because it comes from everywhere' (Foucault 1998 [1976], 93).

Foucault's discussion of power is woven into many of his monographs. From his discussion of the birth of the prison in *Discipline and Punish*, to his research into the history of the notion of madness in *Madness and Civilization*, to his *History of Sexuality* and even his *Archaeology of Knowledge*, the theme of power has had a lasting effect on academia. For Foucault, there is no Power (capital 'P') in the sense of absolute, objective hierarchy. Although smaller hierarchies may exist, power is better characterised by a complex web of power relations. The most insidious form of power is not the direct power of physical domination. Rather, it is the domination that is achieved through the expression of normalised discourse and other discursive formations.

For Foucault 'One needs to be nominalistic, no doubt: power is not an institution, and not a structure; neither is it a certain strength we are endowed with; it is the name that one attributes to a complex strategical situation in a particular society' (Foucault 1998 [1976], 93). Similarly, domination is not 'that solid and global kind of domination that one person exercises over others, or one group over another, but the manifold forms of domination that can be exercised within society' (Foucault 1998 [1976], 96). Foucault looks for intricate expressions of power through insidious means. McHoul and Grace elucidate this further, by outlining that Foucault's conception of power is intelligible in terms of the way it is expressed:

> Many different forms of power exist in our society: legal, administrative, economic, military, and so forth. What they have in common is a shared reliance on certain techniques or methods of application, and all draw some authority by referring to scientific 'truths' ... these techniques ... like any other form of applied knowledge, have a history—and this is what allows for the differentiation of systems of power relations. Foucault's point is to stress that there are no necessary or universal forms for the exercise of power to take place: our society bears witness to the production of quite specific practice which characterise the ways in which power relations function within it. (McHoul and Grace 1993, 65)

For refugees, the expression of power is not necessarily experienced in terms of domination. Small 'p' power is articulated in more subtle ways. These may be explicit, such as working or reporting conditions on visas, or implicit, such as people in a new country not understanding (or not making an effort to understand) their accent. Discourse and power are also closely related, and the entire immigration trajectory is laden with discursive practices and power-imbued discourses. In Australia, the discourse surrounding the threat of radicalisation, and associations made with Islam, has resulted in individuals of "Islamic appearance" being singled out for scrutiny by airport security compared to Caucasians (BBC News Australia 16 March 2015), and in descriptions of 'African Gangs' being disseminated in mainstream media.

A person's capacity for perceiving themselves is necessarily informed by established social practices. However, it is difficult (even perhaps counterproductive) to attempt a stratification of ideological expression; power is always expressed through multiple layers of relations. This means that people are always conceiving of themselves in relation to the categories available to them. For example, the media creates, proliferates, and reinforces notions of subjects such as 'illegal immigrants', 'boat people, 'African gangs', and so on. This process has the potential to become a marker of a collective identity, in the same way that groups of marginalised individuals in the past have taken on board an original derogatory term and made it something to be proud of (such as 'Wog', 'Nigger', etc.). When the media perpetuates the notion that Somali migrants are violent Islamic fundamentalists, a powerful and distinct category is invoked. Somalis are free to decide whether they choose to define themselves in such terms or antithetically. However, the important point here is that they involuntarily consider themselves against the created category. The connection of Islam with terrorism is now embedded in modern Australian society; the formation of categories disseminates through multiple avenues and exemplifies the network of power that can radiate from discourses.

Gen 1.5 Somalis in Melbourne grow up in a culture where many around them (not only individuals within society, but also structures of the society — media, immigration bureaucracy, schools, etc...) view them in terms of the categories prevalent; and if not now, then with the potential of becoming a certain subject with certain properties (such as radicalised). These conceptions do not stem from the subject *a priori*, nor do they cause the subject to respond in a certain way. They are, however, intricately tied up with the subject's perception of the world and orientation within the world and how they are able to orient themselves with respect to the power relations. Nobody grows up in a social vacuum.

◊

The notion of social capital has been popularised in the recent past to the extent that it often forms part of lay discussion regarding identity. This popularisation has blurred the boundaries somewhat between social capital and broader ideas of social connectedness, so it now seems to be understood as an overwhelmingly positive force that enables social interaction and gain.

Social capital is another way of describing the webs of relations that exist in society. Social actors produce and distribute social capital and those with greater social capital are more easily able to advance their own interests, while it is more difficult for those without social capital to do so. It is based on mutual recognition (much like identity and power are) and groups transform objective differences into symbolic differences and classifications. This enables the creation of symbolic distinctions that differentiate groups of people. It is a dynamic and fluid concept of human relations which makes it very difficult to quantify and measure.

Bourdieu defines social capital as 'the sum of resources, actual or virtual, that accrue to an individual or a group by virtue of possessing a durable network of more or less institutionalized relationships of mutual acquaintance and recognition' (Bourdieu and Wacquant 1992, 119). This means that social capital can be found in any social connection or interaction with others. This is most obviously achieved through membership of associations, participation in the workplace and public and government institutions, but equally through more informal networking and interaction. It is not the same as, but intimately connected with, class structures. After all, Bourdieu was interested in how society is reproduced and how the dominant classes retain their position.

What is crucial to Bourdieu's definition of social capital is that it is produced by social actors for their own benefit and distributed in unequal measure. It is therefore a means by which the powerful may further their own interests, often at the cost of those with less.

However, it is important to note that while social capital is pursued for individual or mutual benefit, this pursuit is not always a conscious choice. It may equally arise as a result of activities engaged in by actors for other purposes.

Bourdieu's concept is profoundly linked to notions of class, and greatly emphasises conflicts and the function of power (social relations that allow an actor to advance their own personal interests).

One important characteristic of social capital is that it is based on mutual cognition and recognition. It is from this basis that social capital is transformed into symbolic capital (Bourdieu 1986). Bourdieu argues that groups transform objective differences into symbolic differences and classifications. In this way, groups are able to create symbolic distinctions that differentiate them from other groups. For Bourdieu, it is precisely these symbolic differences, facilitated by social capital, that actualise and legitimate class differences. Otherwise, the social classes are simply classes on paper. 'Symbolic capital ... is nothing other than capital, in whatever form, when perceived by an agent endowed with categories of perception arising from the internalization (embodiment) of the structure of its distribution, i.e. when it is known and recognized as self-evident' (Bourdieu 1985, 204).

In this way, social capital is not something discrete that can be accumulated, rather it is a pervasive force that social actors are all subjected to, knowingly or unknowingly. This can have both positive and negative consequences for social actors. It seems that most social theorists can agree that social capital at its very core relates to the size and availability of networks that a social actor can access. It is 'the ability of actors to secure benefits by virtue of membership in social networks or other social structures' (Portes 1998, 6). These may be qualitatively different, for example, with a large criminal, street or homeless network as opposed to a large ruling class. Furthermore, an essential characteristic of social capital is that it is relational.

> Whereas economic capital is in people's bank accounts and human capital is inside their heads, social capital inheres in the structure of their relationships. To possess social capital, a person must be related to others, and it is these others, not himself, who are the actual source of his or her advantage (Portes 1998, 8).

Thus, social capital exists only when it is shared.

Even though social capital is accessed differently by individual social actors, it can be seen as a collective phenomenon. We can think of bureaucratic organisation as a tool which concentrates social capital. It does so by converting numerous members into an institutionalised, organised accumulation of social capital. Thus, the establishment of a voluntary or community association is also an investment which aims to create networks of relations in order to accumulate social capital (Bourdieu 1986).

In the Australian context, Onyx and Bullen developed a framework to measure social capital for community organisations to assess themselves and their work (Onyx and Bullen 2005 [1997]). They identified a number of factors that contributed to building social capital, including local community participation, feelings of trust and safety, and neighbourhood connections. Ramon Spaaij has applied the concept of social capital to the Somali community in Melbourne using sport as his focus. Spaaij highlights the distinction between bonding, bridging and linking social capital where bonding social capital refers to 'social ties between persons such as relatives, kin, and close friends'. It promotes homogeneity and particularised trust due to its inward-looking nature (Spaaij 2012, 1522). Spaaij explains that for Melbourne Somalis, participation in an ethno-specific football club allows them a means to escape (even if temporarily) social situations that may be fraught with tension, and to be among club members with similar ethnic backgrounds. This creates a safe and relaxed environment for members to come together and strengthen their already established friendships. Many of the young people associated with the club have close friends there, and indeed, became involved with the club because of their friends already playing there. Their participation allows them to rebuild social networks that were disrupted by their experiences as refugees and the war in Somalia. Their social encounters at the club allow them to discuss family and work issues and help each other in everyday life situations (Spaaij 2012, 1527-1528).

Although the majority of the players and position-holders in the club are Somali, there are some players and spectators from other backgrounds (mostly other African countries such as Eritrea and Kenya). Participants in the study argue that social interaction is easier for other Africans in the group because they are similar in ethnicity and colour and are able to feel comfortable together. This is also the case with religion, with a shared Muslim identity also binding members of the club.

◊

This chapter now turns to an exploration of some of the conceptions of violence advanced by anthropologists, ethnographers and social theorists during the modern era. Both overt and covert notions of violence are examined. It discusses in brief the different types of violence that are expressed in response to particular situations and circumstances.

Overt violence is perhaps the most obvious form of violence. It is often described as physical aggression and is expressed in explicit and direct forms. Historians argue that in Europe at least, the practice of open violence peaked in the 1600s, before declining greatly in the mid-seventeenth century, and then again significantly in the mid-eighteenth century (Knafla 2004, 171). Thomas Hobbes described violence in terms of a primeval war of everyman against everyman. Writing in 1651 at the peak of the practice of open violence in Europe, he described nature as a state of war until the influence of civil society takes hold. At the time of writing, he noted that the savage people of America still lived in the grip of this primeval war, not yet having been civilised (Hobbes 1996). For Hobbes, the state of nature is anarchy until we are collectively organised. His view of life without civilisation — 'nasty, brutish, and short' (Hobbes 1996, 78) — justified the supreme authority of the state. This Hobbesian political realism holds that once states are established, the individual drive for power becomes the rationale for the states' behaviour. This, in turn, leads to attempts to dominate other states and individuals. Hobbes' views have inspired modern neoliberal thought and often frame the way in which international relations are discussed (Johnson 1993; Wendt 1999).

Other authors have also noted the decline in violence in parallel with the increase in state control, describing the decline of traditional forms of personal violence, and growth in the state's control of violence through policing. This led to new expectations of social behavioural standards enforced by the state's judicial system, which served to further diminish the culture of personal violence (Knafla 2004, 171).

However, it is difficult to apply these accounts of a decline in violence to the African context (apart from perhaps, the Ottoman empire's influence in Africa). Indeed, overt expressions of violence in the Islamic world have been reported on and disseminated consistently over the last century. As Rashied Omar notes; 'In the contemporary period, Islam is frequently depicted as predisposed to conflict and violence' (Omar 2004, 157). While this is arguably only true of some parts of the Islamic world (it is worth remembering that vast numbers of Muslims reside peaceably in South East

Asia and other places), it certainly seems to reflect the situation in Somalia.

Nuruddin Farah is a well-respected Somali novelist who has documented the naked violence in Somalia, (particularly on the streets of Mogadishu) over more than three decades. In his fictional works, which are strongly rooted in Somali politics, he describes the gun-toting, *qat*-chewing youth who are ready to extinguish human life without provocation and the comfortable, corrupt bureaucrats who make orders that show no concern for civilians and their wellbeing. His descriptions of Somalia, while showing the anarchy and chaos present in all facets of life, also focus on the individuals who are able to manipulate the chaotic situation for their benefit (Farah 2007, 2004, 1998, 1986).

Farah's work shows us in visceral detail how ill-fittting the idea of government as a 'civilising influence' is to Somalia, as there has not been a consistent central governing system to organise and control citizens for decades. Indeed, there is a vocal group of scholars and commentators who argue that stateless societies are highly brutal places. Writing in The New Republic, a conservative American political journal, Steven Pinker states:

> Pre-state societies were far more violent than our own… in tribal violence, the clashes are more frequent, the percentage of men in the population who fight is greater, and the rates of death per battle are higher … If the wars of the twentieth century had killed the same proportion of the population that die in the wars of a typical tribal society, there would have been two billion deaths, not 100 million. (Pinker 2007)

This idea is of particular interest in the context of this study for three reasons. The first is that it seems to be an almost exact echo of the Hobbesian claims, which are more than 350 years old. Secondly, as discussed in section three, there is much to suggest that in fact

Somalia in past centuries has been a remarkably safe place, due to the organisation and social control exerted by the clans (Menkhaus 2004). While it does seem that some of this social order was kept by the judicious use of violence (punishments for taking a life, or for theft or damage of property, for example), this is the sort of violence that modern states have also utilised to keep peace and order. Thirdly, Pinker's assertion that stateless and tribal societies have higher rates of violence relies exclusively on one simple statistical marker: the number of deaths on the battlefield. It does not take into account the myriad other violence types that exist. Equally, one could consider those displaced by conflict, or those who suffer the effects of climate change as measurable forms of violence to add to a statistical figure.

It is possible to identify of many forms of overt violence — such as military violence, intimate partner and domestic violence, child sexual abuse, revolutionary violence, and armed violent conflict. Although there has been a shift in the study of violence towards more covert expressions of violence over the last century or so, the overt forms of violence remain an important dimension for investigating the conceptions and experiences of violence in Gen 1.5 Somalis. Overt violence is a reality the world over, and post-modern studies that attempt, even implicitly, to downplay the primacy and brutality of overt violence miss the mark. Indeed, this research found that many Somalis in Melbourne would not return to Somalia because of the overt violence there.

While violence is often characterised by physical force involving injury or death to persons or damage to property, scholars are increasingly interested in a broader use of the term, extending

> ... beyond the overtly physical to covert, psychological, and institutional violence. In this broader sense racism, sexism, economic exploitation, and ethnic and religious persecution all are possible

> examples of violence; that is, all involve constraints that injure and violate persons, even if not always physically. (Cady 2006, 677).

Thus, covert expressions of violence carry equal weight to overt expressions. In their impressive edited collection *Violence in War and Peace*, Nancy Scheper-Hughes and Philippe Bourgois offer a nuanced definition of violence:

> Violence is a slippery concept—nonlinear, productive, destructive, *and* reproductive. It is mimetic, like imitative magic or homeopathy. "Like produces like," that much we know. Violence gives birth to itself. So we can rightly speak of chains, spirals, and mirrors of violence—or, as we prefer—a continuum of violence (Scheper-Hughes and Bourgois 2004, 1).

While the overt forms of violence are a crucial aspect of theorisations of violence, it is clear that violence is a multifaceted concept, and there are dimensions to it beyond physical aggression. As Scheper-Hughes and Bourgois describe it, 'Violence can never be understood solely in terms of its physicality—force, assault, or the infliction of pain—alone. Violence also includes assaults on the personhood, dignity, sense of worth or value of the victim' (Scheper-Hughes and Bourgois 2004, 1). Assaults on personhood may include violations of reproductive rights, incarceration, prohibition from wearing a preferred form of dress or removal of children from parents.

Along with the explicit forms of violence described earlier, there are also many implicit or hidden forms of violence that are entrenched in human interaction. These include structural violence, which is often invisible because it is so much a part of the routine of everyday life (Scheper-Hughes and Bourgois 2004, 4). A pertinent example of structural violence is the colonial racism and class relations that accompany the acquisition, establishment, exploitation and maintenance of a territory by a coloniser. The unequal relationship between the colonisers and indigenous populations allows structural violence to become ingrained in the interactions between the two in ways that are still being discovered and unravelled today. There is a great deal of scholarship that points to the continuation of this unequal relationship and the structural violence it engenders (Ferguson 2004; Maddison 2014; Jefferess 2008).

Additionally, because structural violence can be more difficult to identify and to rectify it is correspondingly difficult to address (even if class relations and poverty are visible, it is not simple to address them). For example, Scheper-Hughes and Bourgois describe how the explicit physical violence of the apartheid regime, personified by a 'sadistic Boer cop' and his demonstration of torture techniques became a large focus of the South African Truth and Reconciliation amnesty hearings in Cape Town, while the deep structural violence of apartheid which forced 80% of the African population to live in social institutions resembling concentration camps was not examined closely at all (Scheper-Hughes and Bourgois 2004, 1-2).

This kind of pervasive violence fits well with Pierre Bourdieu's ideas. For a thinker such as Bourdieu, violence is everywhere, in everyday social practice. It is rendered invisible or 'misrecognised' because of its constant and unremarkable presence (Bourdieu and Wacquant 1992). Individuals absorb the structures and mechanisms of the societies which they inhabit until they become part of their mental structures (Swingewood 2000, 214). This acceptance of social order (by both those who benefit from it and those who are disadvantaged by it) allows violence to be carried out in plain view without individuals thinking to question it. Similarly, there is a relationship between symbolic violence and performance of other types of violence as a result.

> You cannot cheat with the 'law of the conservation of violence':

> all violence is paid for, and, for example, the structural violence exerted by the financial markets, in the form of layoffs, loss of security, etc., is matched sooner or later in the form of suicides, crime and delinquency, drug addiction, alcoholism, a whole host of minor and major everyday acts of violence (Bourdieu and Wacquant 1992, 40).

◊

The media perform a central role in shaping the way society as a whole sees different groups. This can influence attitudes towards these groups, affect their civil rights and even influence government policy towards them. This in turn may influence the relationship between individual members of those groups and the wider society (Cottle 2004). Other authors have noted 'the tendency of media coverage to position ethnic minorities as problematic others to a white, normative self' (Shohat and Robert 1994). In March 2009, the Australian Human Rights Commission released a report regarding African Australians' experiences of rights and access to key services. One finding of this paper concerned media debates focusing on 'the numbers, "integration potential" and settlement needs of African Australians'. According to the report, the Australian media tend to focus on 'crime or on political commentary about African Australians — and has often been negative or critical, and sometimes misleading' (Australian Human Rights Commission 2009, 7). The following examples relate to violence which has been ascribed to Somalis in Australia. The argument here is that Australian Somalis have been misrepresented through the use of false or misleading statistics which is illustrated by the cases below.

Writing in the *Herald Sun* in 2008, journalist Liam Houlihan claimed that in the twelve months to June 2007, 283 Somali born people committed a crime. Using 2006 census population data, this equates to roughly 1 in 9 (Houlihan 2008). His article provoked a public outcry, and much attention was directed to 'ethnic crime' in the following days. However, as Media Watch pointed out two weeks later, the journalist made a serious mistake in his reading of the crime results released by Victoria Police. He counted the number of offences committed by members of the Somali born population rather than the distinct number of offenders. If a Somali born person was alleged to have committed three offences, in his reading of the statistics, this counted as three separate offenders. Using the statistics correctly, we can see that only 115 alleged offenders were Somali born. This is not 1 in 9, rather 1 in 23 (Media Watch 2008). This number, while still greater than for other nationalities, is significantly closer to the 1 in 31 offenders in the Australian born community as reported by Mr Houlihan (Houlihan 2008).

In 2012, there was widespread anger from the African community when Victoria Police released ethnic crime statistics. These purported to show that Sudanese and Somali-born Victorians were about five times more likely to commit a crime than other Victorians (Oakes 2012). 'The police statistics show the rate of offending among the Sudanese community is 7109.1 per 100,000, while for Somali people it is 6141.8 per 100,000. The figure for the wider community is 1301.0 per 100,000' (Oakes 2012). At a forum organised by African youth representatives and attended by members of Victoria Police, the youth challenged the decision to release the statistics and argued that they were 'incomplete'. At the forum, the police representative also conceded that there may be instances of false identification by criminals contributing to the high statistics, and that because of community attitudes, Africans may be blamed for crimes they did not commit (Reech 2012).

Interestingly, the 2013/2014 crime statistics released by Victoria Police show that the crime rate per 100,000 population was 7489.5 (Victoria Police 2014, 4). This is, in fact, higher than the rates of crime attributed to Sudanese and Somali born Victorians in 2012. It is not known how the police arrived at the 2012 statistics, although their official release documentation states that all the data comes from the LEAP database (Victoria Police 2014). Notwithstanding the community challenges regarding the accuracy and legitimacy of the statistics (and my own concerns regarding the way the statistics were calculated), it is also important to emphasise the productive element of reporting statistics in this way (as detailed in section one).

Young Muslims have been increasingly represented in the media as having the potential to become radicalised. One highly charged area of concern in Australia is the risk of young people becoming attracted to the ideology of the Islamic State (ISIL). There have been some instances of this occuring. For example, in April 2015, a Somali-born Australian was killed while fighting for ISIL. Sharky Jama had been a successful model for over two years, and was well liked and respected within the Melbourne Somali community when he decided to travel to Syria (Schliebs 2015). His death was reported in the context of growing numbers of Jihadis leaving Australia to fight in Syria and other places. However, relatively few media outlets followed the story and reported on the response from within the Somali community in Melbourne. Sharky's father, Dada Jama, said he would speak out with the Somali community and pass on the message to 'look after their kids' ("Melbourne model turned jihadist Sharky Jama shot dead in Syria" 2015). Community leaders have spoken about forming groups against extremism within the Somali community in Melbourne and have urged the government to closely scrutinise the plans of any Australians travelling to areas where ISIL is known to operate ("Sharky Jama, Melbourne male model, reportedly killed fighting with Islamic State in Syria" 2015).

In November 2018, Hassan Khalif Shire Ali drove a truck loaded with gas bottles into central Melbourne, ignited the vehicle and then attacked passers by with a knife. He fatally stabbed one man in the face, and injured two more men. The attacker had a history of minor criminal offences, and had arrived in Australia from Somalia in the 1990s. He was shot by police at the scene and died later in hospital. Islamic State later claimed the attack as one of their own, but there was no independent corroboration of this claim.

A 2015 report released by the Lowy Institute says that the previous Abbott government's 'troubled relations' with Australian Muslim communities hampered efforts to prevent radicalisation and that the significant numbers of Australians fighting in Iraq and Syria represent 'a serious national security threat' (Zammit 2015). The same report points out that while there was a surge in numbers of Australians joining Al Shabaab following the Ethiopian invasion, this appears to have dissipated 'following the disruption of a support network in Melbourne and Al Shabaab's dramatically reduced popularity in the Somali diaspora' (Zammit 2015). The prominence of the perceived threat of radicalisation in Australia is not supported by the Lowy institute's findings. The increased media attention on radicalisation and those 'at risk' is not confined to Australia. For example, Travis Dixon has documented the way terrorism has been reported extensively over the last decade in America. Using the UCLA Communication Studies Digital News Archive, he sampled 146 cable and network news programs aired between 2008 and 2012 to find that Muslims were greatly over-reported as terrorists compared to other groups of people who committed terror offences (Dixon and Williams 2015).

Internationally, there has been increasing attention on international terror attacks, including those carried out by Al Shabaab. Kenya is the most frequent target for Al Shabaab operations, after the deployment of Kenyan troops in the African Union Mission to Somalia. Recent attacks include the 2013 Westgate shopping mall attack, and the 2014 Nairobi bus bombings, Gikomba bombings, Mpeketoni attacks and Lamu attacks. In 2019, Al Shabaab attacked a luxury hotel complex in Nairobi. There has been widespread criticism of the Kenyan government's response to these attacks, which has included mass arrests of the local Somali population. Diplomats and analysts argue that this will create greater divisions and fuel dissent, making radicalisation more likely (Khamis 2015).

Many believe that Al Shabaab has infiltrated Kenya and young Kenyans are being recruited to carry out attacks. There is a large and marginalised Somali-born population in Kenya. In a parallel to the situation in Australia, newspaper reports have noted that 'a huge population of disillusioned youth is vulnerable to radicalisation and recruitment' (Wambua-Soi 2015). There are widespread feelings of disenfranchisement and vulnerability by the Kenyan-Somalis living in the north claiming to be viewed 'with suspicion and as lesser citizens' by the government and fellow Kenyans, and also 'targeted indiscriminately by security forces in terrorism related crackdowns' (Wambua-Soi 2015).

In addition to terrorist activity in Kenya, there was a surge in piracy off the Somali coast. This has declined since 2012, however it remains a threat, and was a high-profile news item between 2008-2013.

> Piracy rose in 2008 by 200 per cent from 2007. Besides hijacking vessels heading west from Asia across the Gulf of Aden to reach Europe, Somali pirates took, in September 2008, 30 hostages on a French luxury yacht who were released for a ransom of about $2 million (Gebrewold 2009, 218).

Reports have described the pirates as ranging from very young and inexperienced, to older and part of a more cohesive group. They are often under the influence of the stimulant *qat*, which makes them edgy and unpredictable (Langewiesche 2009; Verini 2015). The instances of Somali piracy have declined rapidly over the last few years. This is due in part to an upsurge in the successful capture and prosecution of pirates as part of an international effort to halt the hijackings, and to the increasing ability of ships passing through the area to organise and defend themselves (Mohamed 2015).

There are links between the pirates and Al Shabaab (Lough 2011) although these links are not yet fully understood. It is claimed that between 20 and 50% of the ransom money pirates collect is given to Al Shabaab. Pirates also operate out of ports that are controlled by Al Shabaab. They pay rent in cash, or in arms that they have seized (Ibrahim 2010, 290).

While the threat of piracy has eased significantly, violence does continue within Somalia The most significant recent violent attack carried out by Al Shabaab in Somalia occurred on October 14, 2017, when a truck bomb exploded in Mogadishu, killing close to 600 people.

◊

The next section of the book moves away from descriptions of Somalia, Somali Australians, and theoretical notions of identity and invites Gen 1.5 Somali Australians to use their own voices to tell their stories of the lived experience of being young, visibly different members of Australian society.

II – Gen 1.5 in their own words

4

Islam and kinship

Islam is a strong determinant for Somali identity in diaspora (Sporton, Valentine, and Nielsen 2006), and Young Somali Australians are very clear about the importance of Islam in their lives. They discussed it as a personal, social, political, and cultural force and were open about the way their religion affected them and contributed to their identity. Aaliya's statement below is representative of the way many young people discussed Islam with me.

> ***Aaliya:*** *I am a very religious person. I believe that Islam is the best way to live your life and I do my best to follow the ... orders every day.*
>
> *Interview, 21.06.2013*

Mohamed and Ali described it like this:

> ***Mohamed***: *For me, religion is the thing that defines me. It is very important to my family and to me and it's different to the religions you have here (like Catholic, Jew, Hinduism) because it means more to Muslims than other religions mean in Australia. I don't see other people praying like we do.*
>
> ***Ali***: *Yeah, I think religion, you know being Islamic is my... what defines me... yeah, I'm religious, but I think my religion and my beliefs doesn't really prevent me to study or socialise or be like a normal person*
>
> *Group interview, 28.05.2014*

Two interesting perspectives are presented above. Mohamed believes that religion means more to Muslims than other religions do for their adherents in Australia. He highlights the difference between Islam and other religions practised in Australia, and the visibility of the way that Islam is practised. Ali, however, draws a distinction between being religious and being a 'normal person'. He feels a need to point out that his religion and beliefs do not prevent him from engaging in other areas of life.

The physical and practical presence of Islam in the lives of the young Somali Australians was highly noticeable. This was particularly clear at the time of Ramadan, when I mostly ceased contact with the Somali community. However, it was also evident at community events, such as soccer games or cultural festivals. There was a daily observance of prayer, and it was not unusual for people to excuse themselves politely and kneel in a quiet corner to pray. This could be disconcerting in the context of what were sometimes very loud and lively events. Equally, conversations with all generations were peppered with references to Allah. *Insha'Allah* (if Allah wills it) was a common feature in discussions. There was also an acceptance that human actions are defined by the purpose of Allah. I have experienced a similar language and way of being in the company of devout evangelical Christians. One focus of interest of this study was features of religious belief and practice in Australia as it is often claimed that Islam in Somalia is uniform across the country and the practice that most unites the Somali people.

While Somalia has often been presented as a religiously homogenous country, it is important to note that the religious practices across Somalia are not entirely uniform. Sufism permeates the religious practices today, despite consistent efforts by different groups to eradicate it.

Another aspect of Islam that is quite particular is the continued adherence of some Somalis to folk and animist religions. For example, Aaliya described her journey to Somalia in order to be treated with what she described as 'tribal medicine' for a chronic problem with her leg. She was reluctant to give details about what the medicine entailed. This is possibly an example of the folk aspects of the ancient Somali practices being incorporated into modern Somali Islam (Chapin Metz 1992). Aaliya has limited function in both legs and requires a mobility aid to get around. She emphasised that her disability was the result of something foreign in her body which needed to be expelled in order for her to heal. There are doctors in Somalia who practice these healings, and she told me that they live outside the cities. While Aaliya's remaining family in Somalia reside in Mogadishu, she had to drive for five hours outside the city to find a healer. She did not give any details about what occurred during the healing.

> ***Aaliya:*** *I have been back to Somalia a couple of times for my leg. This is not the normal Islam that is practiced in Australia, but a specific sort that belongs in Somalia. I am lucky to be able to return and to visit the tribal medicine doctors.*
>
> *Interview, 21.06.2013*

When asked about how this sort of Islam relates to the 'normal' Islam that in is practiced in Australia, she responded like this:

> ***Aaliya:*** *Yeah, this is an addition to Islam that we Somalis have. But it is all about our relationship with Allah, so it is fine.*
>
> *Interview, 1.06.2013*

Aaliya's story brings to mind some of the mystical elements of Sufism. Sufism is quite widely practiced in Somalia, and it focuses on the inner, transcendent elements of Islam. This emphasises the relationship that adherents have with Allah above all else. Sufism has come under attack in Somalia, with Al Shabaab forbidding its practice and destroying shrines and the graves of saints (*International Religious Freedom (2010): Annual Report to Congress* 2010, 191). Healings such as Aaliya described have often occurred in Sufi practice across the Muslim world although it is difficult to document as it is considered private (Amster 2013, 6; Dominguez Diaz 2015, Chapter 7). In some contexts and countries, it may also be dangerous to identify as Sufi.

This was not the only time the young people described 'additions' to Islam that are specific to Somalia. One other comment that was frequently raised by both males and females was the position of women in Somali households compared with other Muslim communities, which is discussed in greater detail in the next chapter.

In the context of youth engagement with organised religion in Australia lessening quite drastically, it was interesting to hear so many young people describe Islam as the thing that 'defines' them. They were very open about this. However, they also often complained that they were defined by their religion by others.

> ***Ismahaan:*** *This is one aspect of my life, Islam, I mean. It is very important to me, but it is not the only important thing about me.*
>
> *Focus group, 02.11.2012*

In discussing refugee identity, Yuval-Davis highlights the influence that markers of identity have on refugees and their establishment of cultural identities in their new homelands. She focuses on the 'stories people tell themselves and others about who they are (and who they are not)' (Yuval-Davis 2006, 200). She also acknowledges that 'constructions of self and identity can [...] be forced on people' (Yuval-Davis 2006, 202). So the young people felt comfortable in defining themselves by their religion, but were not comfortable for others to do the same thing.

The conflict here seems to occur when situational identity (that which is predominant in face-to-face interactions with others and allows us to mutually construct a definition of the situation is being conflated with their personal identity (that which involves distinctive traits of individuals, such as their name and appearance, personal history and information, personality characteristics, and their special place in a particular kinship network). If personal identity is the identity that defines us as unique individuals, it is an identity that most mainstream Australians are able to keep private if they choose. However, for the Gen 1.5 Somalis, their situational identity (aided by their very visible difference) trumps their personal identity to a mainstream observer and they may feel that their entire identity is subsumed by the fact of their religion. While the understanding of religion as part of the private arena is contested and historically specific, there were often complaints that mainstream Australians have a choice about whether their religion (or lack of religion) is public. Conversely, it is one of the first things noted about Gen 1.5 Somalis due to their dress, physical appearance, and certain religious requirements.

The conversation about religion and its importance often turned very quickly to a worry about how Islam was perceived by mainstream Australian society:

> ***Amal:*** *In terms of religion, it's like any other religion. If somebody is Christian, Jewish, whatever, it's your personal life. It's you and your relationship with God and whatever you believe. And everything else, like everything Somali and Australian, is your culture. It's where you live. And I think my life is pretty similar to yours in terms of work and family and my religion is my private life. So when you see the vision of yourself in the media it's really hard, and you think; 'I'm just like you!'*
>
> *Focus group, 02.11.2014*

When Muslims are (over)represented in the media as potentially violent fundamentalists, a powerful and distinct category is proliferated. In reinforcing notions of Muslims as 'terrorists' or 'radicalised', these ideas become constitutive concepts of experience. This means that when people see Somali Gen 1.5ers in the street, they have a predisposition to view them in a certain way. This causes the young people some distress, and is difficult for them, as it challenges their conception of their own identity.

Hani described how becoming a more observant Muslim changed her brother Ibrahim's life for the better.

> ***Hani:*** *I remember one day, my sister was like, 'Oh Ibrahim, you know what he did one day? We were on the road and there was this dead cat on the street and he stopped it and got out and moved it off the road, got if off the road and then put in in the boot to put it in the bin'. And I was amazed, because anyone would just leave it there, personally, I would leave it there, because, yuk! But he wanted to do the right thing. It was because he was practicing, he was becoming a better person. And I think that personal choice is easier for girls to make. And everyone else like his work friends thought it was a negative thing and tried to convince him out of it.*
>
> *Focus group, 02.11.2012*

Here, both Amal and Hani highlight what they perceive as the private nature of their religious belief in direct contrast to the public nature of the condemnation they receive for their religion. Although Hani says here that she believes it is easier for girls to practice Islam than boys, this was not the consensus, with a number of women pointing out that they are much more visible because they wear hijab.

There were many examples of how Islam improved everyday life in order to illustrate its importance. The young people often highlighted the effect it has on their desire to better themselves and to do good for those around them. This was juxtaposed with their idea that the general opinion of Islam in Australia is very low.

> ***Said:*** *Islam is a wonderful religion. It helps to make you a better person.*
>
> *Group interview, 17.08.2014*

> ***Amal:*** *It's interesting when someone has seen a program for half an hour on SBS and they think they know the whole story of Muslims.*
>
> *Interview, 21.01.2014*

Here, Amal points out that there is a great deal of ignorance regarding Muslims and Islam in Australia. Most of the young people believed that SBS and ABC are the only two national TV channels sympathetic to Muslims and other minority groups. Amal highlights that it takes more than half an hour of watching a program about Islam to understand Muslims. The young people were saddened by the insensitive and ill-informed material regarding Muslims which they believe is presented by the commercial channels.

A recurring theme was that mainstream Australians are likely to assume that Muslims have issues with crime and violence, and to believe that if there are a couple of individuals whose behaviour is unacceptable, that this is representative of the whole community.

> ***Kadiye:*** *I don't get how people can focus on all the negative things that Muslims do when it's actually not that much, statistically. You know, white guys beat their wives up all the time, and they hurt their children and drive badly and kill other people on the road. But there is no 'Aussie crime wave'. But I don't want to be the guy to point that out to my friends, so I just stay quiet about it.*
>
> *Focus group, 10.02.2014*

Kadiye's reflections expose a deep level of prejudice prevalent in mainstream society. By inverting the imagery, and inviting us to consider an 'Aussie crime wave', it becomes clear that this is not something which we would likely hear reported. When a situation is turned on its head, for example, with mainstream Australia viewed through the same lens as Muslim Australians are observed, the implicit power relations become apparent.

Kadiye explained that if the topic came up in conversation at work, he would remain silent or leave the room rather than open a dialogue. When pressed about why he did not feel comfortable talking to his friends about his faith and the way it is represented, he answered simply that he believes he can show people best by being a normal, nice guy and that they will understand that there are bad Muslims just like there are bad Christians and Jews but not all Muslims are like that. Although those were his words, his body language did not match what he was saying, and it seemed that he felt too nervous to discuss this topic with his work mates. He did admit that he did not like to make things serious at work, because:

> ***Kadiye:*** *You know, we're all relaxing, having a good time together. It doesn't need to be political.*
>
> *Focus group, 10.02.2014*

It could be argued that the situation is already political if Muslims are discussed from a position of ignorance or denigrated and Kadiye is not able to address that issue, for fear of what others will think of him. This is a strategic choice in how to handle a particular situation, and Kadiye has chosen not to challenge the assumptions of his work mates, perhaps to keep social relations cordial and unstrained.

Once again, Kadiye's situational identity has overruled his personal identity, to the point where he feels it necessary to leave the room whenever conversations about his faith (an integral part of his personal identity) arise. Kadiye sought to give the impression that he did not mind the way his work mates discussed Islam, and he did not indicate that he had ever been persecuted or made fun of directly, however he became very uncomfortable during this discussion. This was captured in the following field note from the focus group.

> *Kadiye very awkward discussing the way his religion is understood in the work place. I wonder if he feels guilt at not defending his beliefs more? Other members of the group also quiet during this discussion. The tone of the conversation became muted and it took some time for the group energy to bounce back.*
>
> *Field note, 10.02.2014*

◊

Many young people wanted to talk about the shift in behaviour towards them after the September 11, 2001 attacks in The United States.

> ***Hani***: *It's scary. Ever since 9/11, I never used to question my belief at all. I never used to think that Islam taught anything negative. And then 9/11 happened and I was in year 9. Everything changed. People looked at you differently, like you were the enemy. From one day to the next. One day, you were just a normal kid with a scarf. You were odd, yes, but you weren't the enemy. Now, you were the people who didn't belong in this country, the opposite of all the normal people. I felt that so strongly after 9/11. And that was because of the media. And the day after it happened, my best friend had her hijab pulled off while she was going into the bus, and people spat at her. And I thought 'What happened? Why are people being so negative towards us?' 'Til today, I find it really hard when people generalise and jump on the boat of 'Muslims are terrorists, Muslims teach terrorism' and they just don't do any of their own research. I find that really heartbreaking.*
>
> *Focus group, 02.11.2014*

Hani's comments reveal the very personal and intimate effect an event such as 9/11 had on young Muslims living in Australia. She characterises a 'before' and 'after' period in which everything had changed. Interestingly, she admits that before 9/11, while she just felt like a normal kid with a scarf among her peers, she was considered to be 'odd'. However, post the terrorist attacks, she said she felt that she became 'the enemy'. And that she no longer belonged in this country. She was conscious that the public perception of her had altered, although she felt that she had not altered at all.

According to Hani's analysis, this change came about due to the media reportage of the event. Unfair and inaccurate media reportage was a common concern:

> ***Sumaya***: *Because they have that image from the news reports, and they get it from the media and the Internet. These terrible headlines... And you can't really blame the general public for what they think- you see the news and you think 'that could be true' and I just wish people would sit down with us and talk...*
>
> *It's just so unfair that they can write all this stuff that is so wrong. They're always talking about things like 'ethnic gangs' and the problem Muslim youth.*
>
> *Interview, 29.11.2014*

In relation to the gangs, a 1999 study examined the possibility that disenfranchised young Somalis would form groups such as gangs in Melbourne (White et al. 1999). The study focused on those who had experienced poor social integration and disruptions in schooling. The report found that while there were clashes with other youth (particularly those from a mainstream Australian background), the main source of conflict was racial harassment of the young Somalis. They banded together in order to protect each other in the face of the apparent threat. Interestingly, the report found that the young people were strongly committed to Islam and their families and also to Australian institutions. They were also found to be remarkably law-abiding citizens with many future hopes and aspirations despite their difficult pasts. This finding is supported by many later studies on refugee youth, that highlight the importance of faith as a key tenet for newly settled refugees to aid their sense of belonging in Australia (Chen and Schweitzer 2019), and that discrimination against refugee youth can correlate with a range of emotional and behavioural issues, and social difficulties (Jensen, Skårdalsmo, and Fjermestad 2014; Lee, Shin, and Lim 2012). Refugee youth subjected to discrimination and exclusion suffer from poorer mental wellbeing, and are less able to adapt to their new environment (Buchanan et al. 2018; Haffejee 2015).

> ***Amal**: That's what I mean, the journalists don't do research. If you're going to do a story about a group of people... at least just take the time to go and speak with them. Find out about them and who they are and exactly what is going on. Don't speak to one or two people and make up a story about that.*
>
> *Focus group, 02.11.2012*

Bashir believes there is another reason that cultural issues are not adequately reported on in Melbourne.

> ***Bashir**: Well, they could come and do a report, but that would mean that they'd need to visit us, maybe a couple of times even, and there might not be a story at all if they go looking. If they don't bother to look, they have a guaranteed story with all the terrorism stuff.*
>
> ***Suleiman:** The other problem, is that nobody will watch A Current Affair if the story is all about a happy multicultural community doing good things. They want to hear about danger, and they want to know about all the different dangerous people.*
>
> *Focus group, 02.11.2012*

The respondents understood the way that the media shapes public opinion and did not condemn the general public for their perceived tendency to believe what appears in the popular media. Indeed, many of them told me that they believe most people are time-poor and simply do not have the resources to seek out alternatives to popular media.

The idea of 'lazy reporting' was also a common theme in the interviews. There were various reasons offered to explain why reporters rarely get the full story, from the idea that bad news sells and this is what the reporters want to produce, and then the more nuanced understanding that some reporters may be scared of Muslims because of the bad press that already surrounds them.

> ***Cabaas:*** *I find it really hard, you know, because the reporters, other than SBS don't want to come here and find out what we're all about. I really think they might be scared of us because of our difference and that they are affected by all the negative stuff they hear on the news. Which makes it like some kind of circle we'll never break out of.*
>
> *Group interview, 25.08.2014*

The response above shows the belief of the respondents that there is a cycle whereby reporters are reluctant to get close to Muslim communities in Australia, and this reluctance leads to shallow and inaccurate reporting which in turn fuels a further distance between Muslims and the mainstream Australian community. The respondents believed that their misrepresentation in the media means they are mistrusted by the mainstream Australian public.

◊

The association between Islam and terrorism is strong and prevalent in modern Australian society. This discursive formation is disseminated through multiple avenues, most notably the media. I want to spend some time here reflecting on what this means for the identity of the young people who identify as Muslim in Australia today. A number of identity theories have been utilised in order to examine the expression of Gen 1.5 Somali Australian identity. At the innermost level, John Hewitt's tripartite consideration of identity has been used. The next layer out concerns the accrual and dispersal of social capital. In the Bourdieuian sense, social capital greatly emphasises class and the idea that the way individuals experience social capital will be markedly different depending on their gender, age, class, and ethnic background. This kind of social capital is conceived here as the operationalisation of the next level of force, which impacts the identity of the respondents. This is Foucault's small 'p' power. This power, which is present for all social actors is characterised by a complex web of power relations exercised through the expression of normalised discourse and other discursive formations.

While this model is likely applicable to any individual and the struggle to express and maintain their identity, it would be significantly more challenging for Gen 1.5 Somalis to do so because the same forces that act upon all social actors are stronger for them. For example, in terms of John Hewitt's tripartite definition of identity, their situational identities are deeply informed by what others know and assume about them. This is of course, true for any social actor. However, Gen 1.5 Somali Australians approach interactions suspecting or knowing that others are likely to have already constructed a certain opinion of them. This informs their expectations and interpretations of their own and others' behaviour. Similarly, their social identities are intricately tied up in being members of a visible group, based on age, ethnicity, and religion. Personal identity concerns the efforts of an individual to construct and preserve their personal narrative, which helps to establish a sense of difference from others. This includes their distinctive traits (again, many of which are highly visible). Goffman suggests that personal identity involves personal history and appearance and a special place in a kinship network. These markers were all described in detail by my participants. Another way to think of the struggle that Gen 1.5 Somali Australians face in maintaining a coherent sense of identity is to consider that there is greater distance between the different selves of these young people than for many other social actors. In this sense, they must bring together more disparate identities, and under more intense scrutiny than is the norm.

Stepping out to the next sphere of influence, the notion of social capital in a Bourdieuian sense is also particularly relevant. There is a close connection between social capital and class, which was found to be particularly relevant to Somali Gen 1.5ers in Melbourne. This was expressed in a number of ways. Firstly, the people interviewed were largely from middle to upper-middle class families in Somalia. There is evidence of this in the relatively high educational attainment of their parents (and in some cases, grandparents). Respondents agreed that those people who were better educated and employed were the first to be able to leave Somalia around the time of the outbreak of the civil war. Thirdly, the respondents believed that there was a hierarchy of ideal destination countries for Somali refugees. While European countries apparently ranked highest, Australia was also high on this list, ahead of Asian countries and other African countries. Therefore, it can be assumed that the respondents in this study were better connected in Somalia (according to them being able to settle in Australia required more money and connections than settlement in another African country, for example). Thus, it can be assumed that these families have experienced a downward shift in social status between Somalia and Australia. I believe that one strategy employed to deal with this situation is to become quite an inward-looking and independent group, which sets itself apart from other groups.

Similar findings have been published regarding Somalis residing in London. The authors identify that Somalis ‘have a tradition of self-reliance and communal solidarity that often conflicts with their exiled status as passive recipients of welfare benefits' (Harding, Clarke, and Chappell 2007, 6). This self-reliance has both positive and negative aspects. For example, one outcome is the focus on young people and the need for them to improve their life circumstances. The older generation believe this has pushed young people to achieve well in their education and entry to the labour market. However, some young people feel pressured by the expectations upon them and would prefer not to face such intense scrutiny from their (well-meaning) parents and grandparents. Another outcome is that there is a reluctance to engage with social services, due to Somali Australians' preference to look to other members of their community for support when dealing with difficult situations. Indeed, there are many examples of these community connections proving successful in managing social, financial, and personal problems. However, there is limited knowledge of and willingness to engage with relevant external services which might be of assistance when necessary.

The next level of the identity model focusses on Foucauldian small 'p' power. The complex strategic situation referred to by Foucault is further complicated by a number of other factors. First there is the difficulty in being Gen 1.5 and straddling very different cultures. Secondly, there is a visible difference due to ethnicity and religion. Thirdly, the refugee experience has meant disrupted schooling, the need to learn another language quickly, loss of family social capital and the structural disadvantage in many aspects of life in Australia, such as access to the labour and housing market.

The Gen 1.5ers in this study are walking a delicate tightrope, however they must also contend with their identities being conflated with a larger misconception surrounding Islam. Ghassan Hage has consistently argued that 'Australia still comprises a predominantly white, Christian society, currently characterised by an increasing fear of different ethnic groups' (Hage 2003). This was touched upon in many discussions by the young people, most often in relation to media representation.

When asked why they thought there was such a strong focus on Islam in the media and from the general public, there were varied answers. Omar described it as a simple result of the attention being focussed on the latest migrants to arrive in the country:

> ***Omar***: *We arrived here last, and you know, there aren't really that many of us, compared to the Italians and the Greeks.*
>
> *Group interview, 11.05.2014*

The small numbers of Muslims and their visibility was a common theme.

> ***Absame***: *When I walk around, people know straight away that I'm different. I can't change the colour of my skin. You know, in Heidelberg it's almost normal because we all live together, but as soon as I catch a train or a bus somewhere, I'm the one that sticks out again.*
>
> ***Kadiye***: *It's weird because in my family we have really strong friendships with our neighbours and aunties and uncles so it's like we could go on forever not really knowing any Anglo Aussies. But when I started my trade, that changed really fast. The rest of the boys are all white and even though they're really good guys, it takes a long time to feel comfortable.*
>
> *Focus group, 10.02.2014*

Kadiye previously commented that he did not wish to enter conversations at work when the topic of Islam and Muslims came up, preferring to leave the room and keep peace with his colleagues. He professed not to care about this, but his comments show that he has experienced tension in the workplace because of his visible difference.

While the young people painted a very positive picture of Islam for them in their personal lives, they also offered explanations as to why the religion is viewed with suspicion and how it can be practiced improperly.

> ***Naado**: And the people who follow Islam in an oppressive country and want to escape it, they want to escape the implementation of the religion, and not the religion itself. This is a problem with society, not the religion. If the society implements the religion badly, people will want to escape and to feel free.*
>
> *Interview, 06.06.2014*

Naado had reflected deeply on what Islam means to her on a personal level and the way that the religion has been practiced in different times and places. She was eager to discuss the way that Islam is practiced in countries she has visited or has some connection to. Naado is an intelligent and articulate young woman, and she was one of the few respondents to draw a distinction between the implementation of religion and the religion at its heart. One area of strong interest to her was the wearing of hijab.

◊

Naado explained to me that she had considered not veiling herself in her late teens after she finished high school and started university. She had not told friends about her deliberations, and she did not give the impression of having agonised over her decision. Rather, it seemed that she felt a duty to question this aspect of her life and examine her beliefs before continuing to veil herself.

One of the mixed gender focus groups yielded interesting discussions about wearing hijab and what it means to Somali women.

> ***Mohamed**: Yeah, I don't know any girls that don't wear hijab. I don't think it would be allowed to be honest.*

> ***Bilan:*** *All the women in my family wear hijab. I remember being really excited when I was little to be able to do that, too. It was really something I looked forward to, because it would show I had reached my maturity.*
>
> *Focus group, 25.08.2014*

It is difficult to draw conclusions about increased religiosity in the Somali community in Melbourne, although a number of studies have highlighted increased religiosity in diasporic communities across the world (Herberg 1960; Garcia-Muñoz and Neuman 2013; Van Tubergen and Sindradottir 2011). Some of the young people reported that they felt their religion had been tested by being a minority religion and was stronger as a result. However, others spoke about the way that religion in general is not very important in Australia and thus, Islam featured less in their personal lives. Some young men reported that Islam is not important to them but that they 'go along with it' to keep their parents happy.

When the discussion turned to the way hijab is perceived in Australia, Hani had this to say:

> ***Hani****: I find the whole notion of being free and not wearing the hijab really ridiculous. This is my freedom — the opportunity to wear my hijab is my freedom. If there was a ban on hijab today, I would move out of this country. Because that is oppression. I think a lot of people don't know what freedom is.*
>
> ***Elizabeth****: Would you go back to Somalia?*
>
> ***Hani****: It doesn't matter where, just somewhere I would be able to practice my religion the way I believe is the right way.*
>
> *Interview, 22.09.2014*

This comment did not have the air of a flippant observation. Hani was very serious about her desire and right to dress as she chooses. Her allegiance here is to Islam and the freedom to practice her beliefs rather than to Australia. She is clear that it is more important to her to be able to practice Islam than it is to remain in Australia. For Hani, commitment to Islam takes primacy over commitment to any nation. She clearly stated her priority is the ability to practice her religion in the way she believes is right.

Bilan discussed the way that others acted towards her based on nothing more than her wearing of hijab.

> ***Bilan:*** *It's so weird, because it's like the only thing they see about me. They don't recognise me as a woman, as a nurse, as a sister or daughter. They just think 'Oh, she's Muslim'. That used to make me really angry. Really angry and upset, but one of my colleagues at work sat with me one day and helped me to see..., she explained that that means their reaction to me is more about what the hijab means for them.*
>
> *Interview, 19.05.2013*

There is an immediate tension for women who wear hijab, as it has come to be treated as a symbol of the supposedly negative aspects of Islam and as a sign of the potential of Muslims to subvert social cohesion (Ho 2007). The hijab can be likened to what Goffman would describe as a 'stigma'; an undesired attribute which is deeply discrediting and which allows us to believe that the person with the stigma is 'not quite human' (Goffman 1963, 5). If the hijab is a stigma which represents Islam, then observers feel that the person wearing the hijab is inferior, and identified only by her religion. This was touched upon many times by the women, who felt very strongly that their wearing of the veil caused others to see them as inferior. I also observed evidence of this on many occasions, most often while on public transport. When veiled young women got onto public transport there was often a reaction from others in the carriage, or on the bus. This ranged from surreptitious looks directed at the veiled women, to conversations dying down and quite obvious stares.

I did not witness any verbal or physical abuse, although there were stories of women who had been spat on or shoved out of the way, as well as those who had been ordered to 'go home' and get out of Australia. Many recent reports have indicated an increasing prevalence of racist attacks on Muslim women (particularly on public transport) (Taha and McDonald 2014; Battersby 2015). The Islamophobia Register in Australia has compiled reports of abuse of Muslims since September 2014 and has documented spikes in these reports after incidents which bring terrorism to public attention (for example, the Martin place siege in Sydney, or anti-terrorism raids in Brisbane) (Battersby 2015).

Bilan's discussion with her colleague reveals a level of perspicacity regarding the idea that this stigma reveals more about those who cannot look past it than about she herself. As observers have chosen to focus on the stigma, and the presumed inferiority of the person wearing it, their fear may make it difficult to inform them about Islam and Muslims, which will allow them to continue to be close-minded and remain unchallenged in their beliefs.

Nafiso described her hijab as an outward expression of her commitment to Islam.

> ***Nafiso:*** *This is the thing that shows the world that I follow Islam. It is an important part of who I am. I get it if other people don't want to wear it. That's fine by me. But I don't go around judging other people's clothes. No, it's not something I would wear, but I'd never make rude comments about them. I think everyone should be able to wear what they want.*
>
> *Interview, 25.01.2014*

Nafiso understood that while the hijab is a symbol of her faith for her, it represents different things to different people. Many of the young women lamented that their wearing of the veil made their religion a matter of public consumption. They were adamant that they would like their religious practice to remain private (a luxury which they believe is afforded to people of many other religious faiths), but at the same time, they were clear about their choice to remain veiled. Removing their veils in order not to attract unwanted attention was not an option.

While Nafiso was not concerned with other people's decisions regarding modes of dress, some of the young men I spoke to were concerned about their exposure to women in dress they considered immodest.

> ***Said**: When I'm at work, and some of the apprentices' girlfriends come, I can't believe the things they're wearing. I just try to not look at them and keep going with the job. They tease me sometimes about it but I don't feel comfortable...*
>
> ***Cabaas**: I wouldn't be happy if my sisters were dressing like that [the way white Australian women dress]. I don't think it's good for anyone to go around wearing [revealing] clothes like that.*
>
> ***Elizabeth**: When you say anyone, do you mean men and women?*
>
> ***Cabaas**: Yeah, both.*
>
> *Focus group, 10.11.2012*

Interestingly, the young men thought it was equally important for them to be modest as for the women. However, they also felt entitled to judge women based on their dress according to their own religious code.

> ***Cabaas:** Yeah, everyone does their best to follow Allah and the prophet, but we're human too. We make mistakes, or some people don't believe in all of the religion. It's like saying that everyone who lives in Australia doesn't have sexual relations before they get married because that's what the Christian church teaches. And the Jewish religion too.*

Group interview, 25.08.2014

It seems ridiculous to assume that all inhabitants of Australia abide by the ancient rules of their religion, but this is the sort of reportage that young Muslims in Australia hear about themselves every day. Consider how it might look if we assumed that any Australian who identifies as Christian must believe in original sin, never have pre-marital sexual relations, abstain from getting any kind of tattoo, and so on. It is perhaps better understood in Australia that identifying as Christian does not mean automatically agreeing with every Christian tenet of faith, as the existence of LGBTIQ ministers in some Christian denominations evidences. Practicing Christians are able to have liberal social views, while adhering to their faith in a way that suits them. It would be absurd to measure mainstream Australians by strict and inflexible religious standards which do not appreciate the diversity of lived religious expression. And yet this is a common occurrence for young Muslims. A very clear indication of the double standard at play can be found in the community outrage that greeted Israel Folau's homophobic statements in 2018 that gay people will go to hell. These statements were rooted in Folau's faith, but this extreme version of Christianity is not acceptable in broader society, and not indicative of the beliefs of all Christians in Australia.

Wearing hijab is a fitting example of the way the young women I met practice Islam in a significant and physical way. In their decision to veil every day, they are committing themselves outwardly and physically to their religion. This commitment comes in the face of significant pressure from some mainstream Australians, including verbal and physical abuse in some cases.

The young people were vocal about the importance of Islam in their lives, and on the whole, they believed that it sets them apart from both mainstream Australians, and other ethnic minorities. They described the difficulties they encountered when their religious identities were questioned by mainstream Australians, although some were more willing to defend themselves than others. The importance of Islam to their identities was continually underscored.

It was interesting to compare this engagement with Islam with a lack of engagement with another cultural and social force: the Somali clan system. Many of the young people were anxious to distance themselves from the clans and to play down the importance of the clans to their identities.

◊

The question of clan kinship comes up with striking regularity in discussions about Somalia and Somali culture. This is true from the very early anthropological texts about Somalia to the latest reports detailing the political situation there, and many items in the popular media. In fact, the clans seem to be the most recognisable attribute of the country. Mention is made of the clans to differentiate Somalia from other African nations facing similar humanitarian crises.

According to Aden Ibrahim, president of the Somali Cultural Association, clan divisions are still prevalent in Melbourne (Cited in (Warne-Smith and Wilson 6 August 2009). His statement is backed by other research (J. Smith 2008, 50). Ramon Spaaij also emphasises the fragmented nature of the Somali social landscape in Melbourne and points to clan divisions as contributing to this fragmentation. He argues that 'Clan divisions have been particularly salient at the level of community associations that compete for power and funding' (Spaaij 2012, 1525).

I spoke with a public defender at Legal Aid who related two separate incidents where Somalis on trial for criminal offences required an interpreter. In both cases, the trials had to be stopped as the interpreters could not refrain from adding their own remarks to the statements they interpreted from the defendant. They both questioned the trustworthiness of the two defendants based on their clan member ship, making comments like: *He says he was not in the area on the Saturday night in August, but I wouldn't believe what he says, because he is from the *** clan, and you can't believe anything they say.* This is clear evidence of the clan divisions which are still pertinent in Melbourne today.

Given the consistency and the depth of the discussion surrounding the Somali clans, I expected the topic to be raised in our conversations. Interestingly, in the individual interviews, none of the respondents brought the topic up until a direct question about clans or the political situation in Somalia was asked. When the topic was raised, responses were well considered and many included an element of political or social analysis regarding clan function in Somalia.

> ***Elizabeth:*** *So what can you tell me about clans in Somalia?*
>
> ***Absame:*** *The clans is like... an ancient system to divide up the country's people into groups where they have a duty [to each other]. It can get pretty dangerous if one clan feels insulted by another one, like if someone doesn't get a job they applied for in an organisation that's part of a clan. They all start to argue and it escalates pretty quick.*
>
> *Focus group, 10.02.2014*

Absame's observation highlights the ancient nature of the clan system as a form of territorial governance, and the way that it functions based on mutual allegiance. The example he offered of the clan's protection of its members was a common theme among the respondents. This is also very commonly described in academic and political writing as the main function of the clans. They have been described as 'social insurance cooperatives' (Hesse 2010,

251). However, the academic description of clans is steeped in ancient nomadic settings, with discussion of dowries, camels as currency and competition for water to survive in the desert (Abdullahi 2001; Aidid and Ruhela 1994; A.H. Ali 2010; Lewis 1994, 2002). Compare this ancient rural imagery with some of the examples the young people gave which take place in urban or commercial settings.

> ***Cabaas:*** *So if you are in a different clan, you might not get a job with a company where the director is from another clan. And if you do get that job, you might not be able to move up very high in the company.*
>
> *Group interview, 25.08.2014*
>
> ***Suleiman:*** *My uncle, he wanted to open a shop, a business in the central district in Mogadishu after the civil war, but he couldn't find somewhere to rent in that district because it was controlled by another clan. I don't even know who it was in charge, but they wouldn't rent any buildings to him; not even a tiny room in an office.*
>
> ***Ali:*** *It's hard to get ahead unless you have those clan connections looking after you.*
>
> *Focus group, 10.02.2014*

The young people very clearly identified the clan system as a form of social capital. They stated that in Somalia it was difficult to be successful without clan connections and described the clans as a web of relationships that included everybody somehow. While they did not describe any of the ancient clan practices such as taking revenge for murder (something which is very often referred to in the literature), they did talk about how the clans support members if they are in trouble financially or in business.

The clan system can be considered as a form of social capital as conceived by Bourdieu. Far from being a system that accords every member equal opportunity, the clans emphasise the inherent power and inequality that is present in social capital. Again, Bourdieu's definition of social capital as 'the sum of resources, actual or virtual, that accrue to an individual or a group by virtue of possessing a durable network of more or less institutionalized relationships of mutual acquaintance and recognition' is most fitting (Bourdieu and Wacquant 1992, 119).

The clan system is an ancient institution in Somalia. It can be interpreted as a system of social capital, which is generated each time a person subscribes to that institution in order to make a social, familial, financial or political connection. However, the clans are not simply an ancient kinship organisational system — the situation is far more complex. For example, the respondents argued variously that clan conflict is responsible for the continued failure to establish a central government in Somalia, linked to pirates and their activities, and the reason their parents fled Somalia.

In a Foucauldian sense, we can use the clan system as a lens to examine the way that ideology permeates individual actors across space and time. It allows individuals to orient (and re-orient) themselves in relation to the unspoken, implicit structures of Somali society and historical roots. In this reading, clan discourse has been so ingrained in Somali identity that it acts as an implicit interpolation. However, it is important to note that the young people did not raise the topic of clans independently. They seemed to be distancing themselves from the social organisation that was the norm for their parents and grandparents in Somalia.

Kadiye's opinion about the origin of the clan system reflected the nomadic and pastoral history of Somalia, but also the way that the clan system has been taken advantage of:

> ***Kadiye:*** *I think the tribes existed because Somali was like, a really*

hard place to live. The climate and the weather is hard and the people got together for protection and to help each other, like a security net. So that's one side of it. Another side is that it was exploited by colonial powers or people who were supposed to be doing aid instead. And they tried to focus on the differences between the clans and make a wedge between people who used to be friends.

Focus group, 10.02.2014

This is in agreement with much of the published material about the clans, regarding the harshness of the environment of Somalia and the need for safety in numbers. However, Kadiye (along with many other commentators) emphasises that this human security net has been manipulated by outsiders to their own advantage.

Sumaya had different ideas about the origin of the clan system.

***Sumaya**: I think it was more of a systematic kind of thing that was put in place, probably from the colonial power or whatever, I don't know. My dad talks about it!*

Interview, 05.05.2013

She clearly does not believe the clan system to be as ancient as Absame does. Italy (the colonial power she refers to) did not have much involvement in Somalia before the early 20th century. When I pressed her on the existence of clans before the colonial power implemented the system, she replied that yes, of course it must be the case, because:

***Sumaya:** I remember other kids reciting the line of the family when I was younger, and it went on for a very long time!*

Interview, 05.05.2013

She is describing the ritual recitation of the family tree, which some families consider very important. Sumaya told me that for some families, this recitation can go hand in hand with Qur'anic recitation and is similarly expected to be done by heart.

Some respondents offered positive descriptions of the clan system.

> ***Nafiso****: The clans are there for when you get into trouble. Maybe you have debt, or your business is not going well. Or maybe your kid did a crime and you need help to go to the courts or get him out of jail...*
>
> *Focus group, 15.01.2014*

When the question was asked at a focus group if the clans carried any influence in the legal system in Somalia, there was a general agreement that they did, although this was not the case in Australia. The group went on to discuss the positive and negative aspects of the clans at length.

> ***Hani****: In some ways it helps, but the negative side obviously is, when someone, say you're from a particular tribe and another tribe which is more common and affluent in that area is killed by a minor person, then that person would retaliate and come and start a war against this person. So it's like a back and forth issue of fighting and killing because one people (sic) died. And the pride they have – I think it's more a pride issue when they say 'Why did you kill our people, this is our blood?' And this is what led to the war in Somalia.*
>
> ***Amal****: Yeah, because tribes have always existed and the way it was used was assisting, helping each other and developing communities, but it wasn't actually meant to cause problems but people and their lack of education...*
>
> *Focus group, 02.11.2012*

The clan system offers a clear way to identify and understand actors' places within a network of relations. While there are no distinct modes of dress or jewellery that distinguish members of clans (Stanton 2003), the respondents said their parents could usually tell who belonged to which clans. This information is apparently readily proffered, and most people do not need to ask. However, this is not a foolproof or completely accurate identification, and mistakes are made in ascribing kinship.

The young people mobilised the clan system themselves as an explanation for the circumstances in Somalia, and of Somalis who have emigrated elsewhere. Ramon Spaaij's findings that the Somali Australian community in Melbourne is divided by clans and that these divisions prevent successful representation in the fight for social and financial resources have already been discussed (Spaaij 2012). Similarly, in London, one study found that clan divisions have remained prominent and have weakened the community's ability to pursue collective projects (Griffiths 2002). However, this is by no means a universal occurrence among Somalis living abroad. Mulki Al-Sharmani has argued that Somalis in Cairo have emphasised the need for unity and cooperation, and that they explicitly contrast this to the clan conflict in Somalia (Al-Sharmani 2007). In the same edited volume, Cindy Horst points out that while Somalis living in Minneapolis tend to remit only to their particular networks, there are no significant clan divisions in the city (Horst 2007). This suggests that clan divisions are not a fixture of Somali identity, rather that they are a response to certain specific circumstances. The responses above also clearly indicate that Hani and Amal believe that the clan system is somewhat incompatible with modern life. Hani describes how it led to the civil war, while Amal equates it with a primitive time, when people lacked education.

The young people frequently referred to the problems the clan system causes, while acknowledging that there are positive aspects also.

> ***Amal**: So we never ever discussed it at all. It never comes into the conversation other than us bagging it or saying how much it causes*

problems. But we actually we're never taught that at a young age so when I was older I found out the good side of tribes, which is you know, people assisting one another, people recognizing where you're from, even though you're in a different part of Somalia.

***Sumaya**: I found out my cousin, she's my second cousin actually, was one of my friends. We were talking about our grandfather and we realised it was the same guy. So it's good in some ways.*

Focus group, 02.11.2012

Of particular interest is that none of the participants ever identified themselves as belonging to a particular clan or lineage without being asked directly. The below excerpt of a group conversation is a good example.

***Elizabeth**: Now, when I've spoken to a lot of older people, they've talked about what clans are and what an important part of life they are.*

[Group reacts]: Ew!

Oh!

Here we go...

***Elizabeth**: And when I've spoken to young people, I've had [the above] reaction. So I wanted to gauge what you think about the clan system.*

***Sumaya**: I didn't even know my tribe until I was second year of university.*

***Amal**: I think it's absolutely irrelevant.*

***Hani**: The thing is, at a young age, my parents actually never taught us our tribe. They never gave it any importance to us as kids — especially living in Australia. My dad is the one that's totally against teaching us our clan, but my mother said 'you should know who you're from and who are your people.' So at a young age I remember my aunty coming to my house and saying 'can you* *count from generations what the names of your clan are?' and she used to teach us. And my dad would hear and say 'Don't teach my kids that'. And so at a young age, we thought it was something bad. I personally thought it was something that caused wars and was difficult and hard and it was just something negative to me.*

***Elizabeth**: So do you know what clans you belong to?*

***Sumaya**: Yeah, but do we really have to go into it?*

Focus group, 02.11.2012

Sumaya's frustration at being asked about her clan identity was palpable. In the course of the discussions with the young people, while there was a high level of knowledge of clan systems, the question began to arise if they were distancing themselves from the clans partly in order to differentiate themselves from their parents and the previous generation. Some of them said explicitly that the clan system does not belong in Australia and that it is not useful anymore. This was in direct contrast to the opinions of older Somali Australians who believed strongly that clans are important and useful in both Somalia and Australia.

Interestingly, the family tree recitation described above by Sumaya was expressly forbidden in Hani's house, although there was some disagreement between Hani's parents about the importance of clan knowledge for children. Some of the older people believed that it was important for the younger generations (those who have spent much of their lives outside Somalia) to understand and take part in this ritual in order to know their place, and where they come from. For them, the ritual recital of clan lineage serves to orient young people in their personal, familial, and national history.

What characterised the discussions about the clans was an initial strong reticence to speak about the topic, followed by in-depth discussion about the influence the clans have had in Somalia once the conversation was flowing. However, this influence was described at arm's length, in reference to parents and grandparents. The young people very rarely reflected on the impact of the clans on their own lives. Some of them were not even aware of which clan they belonged to until they reached adulthood as described by Sumaya above. As Hani describes, she only found out her clan lineage by accident:

> ***Hani:*** *...and then at an older age, when I found out about my tribe at Uni.*
>
> ***Elizabeth****: Did you ask about that, or did it just come up?*
>
> ***Hani****: Well the thing is, it was by accident that it came up because none of my friends are the same tribe as me. But one of them made a mistake and assumed she was. So I went home that night and asked my Mum about it for the first time.*
>
> *Interview, 20.01.2014*

The majority of respondents believed that there were some young Somalis who found the clan lineage important, although these people were not held in particularly high regard. It seemed that the Generation 1.5ers were linked by their professed disregard for the clans. They sought to identify themselves as different from their parents, the first-generation migrants. The majority of older Somalis in Melbourne had positive stories about the clans and how they are there to help when people experience difficult times. (Although, there were some — such as Hani's father —who have disassociated from the clans completely.) The young people had been exposed to the clan system in Somalia for long enough to have personal memories of it, and it is still something that is important to their parents in Australia. Many older men and women were proud of the clan system and told stories of how it had benefitted them in Somalia and in Australia (helping them to find employment, housing, or getting them out of financial trouble).

> ***Ismahaan**: Some people still have arguments about it! I sit there and I'm like 'Yep, I know what I am and that's all that matters'.*
>
> ***Amal**: it's still an issue amongst people in our age group who really feel like because they're a certain tribe they're superior. They have this feeling. It exists in Somalia and it exists here. I just don't know why. Because the clans aren't really in place here, you know?*
>
> *Focus group, 15.01.2014*
>
> ***Said**: It depends who you hang around with. Personally, I don't care about the clans very much. But I know my parents still do.*
>
> *Group interview, 17.08.2014*

Hani's father did not like to have the clans discussed in the house when she was growing up. Hani believed this was positive.

> ***Hani:** It's sad, because I thought everyone didn't know, that everyone else was like me. I think the clans are completely irrelevant.*
>
> *Interview, 20.01.2014*

But it became obvious that what the young women were saying did not entirely match the information divulged in discussions. On the one hand, they stated that the clan system was 'completely irrelevant' to them, but on the other they had lengthy discussions on the subject of clans.

Similarly, Hani highlighted that she did not even find out her clan lineage until university and only then by accident, but the way the accident arose was through her friend assuming that she was part of the same clan and questioning her about it, which indicates that her friend, at least, found lineage important. Ismahaan described how it is important for her to know who she is 'and that's all that matters'. So the identity conferred by clan-belonging is actually important to her, even if she says she does not care what other people think, or care what clan others belong to. The young people seemed to be taking control of their current circumstances by distancing themselves from a clan system that had not offered them anything in terms of help in distress. Rather they viewed it as an old-fashioned system which had no use for them in their lives in Australia.

It took a number of focus groups and individual interviews for the realisation to set in that there seemed to be some discrepancy in the data collected on the young people's impressions of the clan system. It was difficult, because once asked, they were all happy to talk about the subject. However, the topic was always required to be raised before it could be discussed. Something that initially surprised me (and then made me suspicious after I had heard the same story over and over) was that they professed not to care at all about the clans, but were able to offer well thought-out answers to my questions on the topic. These answers had obviously been discussed before, and not thought up 'off the cuff'. It was also interesting that what the young people reported was quite different to what people of their parents' generation reported, and there was a sense that they had discussed the clan system privately amongst themselves as well as with older people. Finally, the length of the discussion about clans after the topic had been raised was surprising. They had lots to say, and truly wanted me to understand their perspective on the clans. For these reasons, I began to suspect that their dismissive stance on clans was not all it seemed.

There are several possible reasons for the young peoples' professed disinterest in the clan system, which is in direct contrast to the importance placed on clans by older community members. One reason the young people did not want to identify with the clan system was perhaps that they recognise that it is called upon to explain many of the negative circumstances in Somalia. They do not wish to be considered primitive or old fashioned, instead locating themselves in their "new" culture and looking forward, rather than being associated with a "backwards practice".

It is also likely they were purposefully distancing themselves from their parents' faith in the clans in order to identify themselves as different from their parents' generation. Another possible explanation for this indifference might be that all the young people in this study were either studying or working and were living with their parents. Due to the support of their immediate families, and the relatively few financial and professional pressures they have experienced, it is possible that they have not needed to draw on the support of the clans. Perhaps if the young people had more exposure to financial, personal, and professional pressures, they would be forced to rely on their clan networks more heavily. Equally, while the support system offered within the Somali Australian community seems strong, there are limits to the extent of connections a newly arrived refugee group can achieve in the decades since settlement in Australia began. While these connections were well established and regularly called upon in Somalia, the scope for what can be achieved in Australia based on such connections is limited.

The importance of the clan structure is not something at the forefront of Generation 1.5 identity. Their identity and social existence have been conditioned by spending their youth in Australian society. They do not view the clan system as a vital part of life in the way their parents do. For their parents, on the other hand, the vagaries of their historical trajectories mean that many will have relied on their clans in the past, and still feel a great sense of connection to them today. Nevertheless, if Gen 1.5ers were to travel back to Somalia and live for a period of time under greater hardship with distant family connections, they might begin to see the relevance of the clan system for themselves. Even if the clan structure is dismissed as irrelevant by many of the participants, they *do* know about it. It exists dormant in the background — in their own personal narrative histories — and is thus still a part of their constructed identities.

So the clans are certainly present in the minds of the young Somalis, even if they stress that clans do not mean much to them. There was, however, no strong agreement about the history of the clans, or about their current incarnation as exemplified in the conversation below:

> ***Ismahaan***: *I always knew what tribe I came from but never really in depth. I didn't learn the sub, sub, sub tribes.*
>
> ***Sumaya***: *When you describe it there's one common one and from that a sub one and a sub from that and so on. It's like a family tree.*
>
> ***Hani***: *I think there's two different clans, the Darod and the Hawiye.*
>
> ***Sumaya***: *There's many*
>
> ***Hani***: *Oh yeah?*
>
> ***Ismahaan***: *There's all these other ones! And each speaks its own dialect. There's heaps of other ones.*
>
> *Focus group, 02.11.2012*

Regional differences within countries including particular dialects and practices are of course not uncommon. However, it is difficult to think of other regions and countries where individuals who share a relationship are required to take certain formalised steps in response to different events including marriage, blood payments when a clan member has committed some kind of offence, grazing rights and ritualised recitation of kinship lines. According to Hesse, not all Somalis agree to which lineage other Somalis belong. As Somali genealogy presents so many ways to affiliate with or disassociate from fellow Somalis, Hesse even argues that this may be the point of the genealogy system (Hesse 2010, 249). So the young people's confusion is understandable, given the lack of certainty about lineage. This is also because certainty is established through practice. While Islam is practiced daily in a physical sense, the clans are understood through family knowledge, but have a much more limited practice among the young people.

In the meetings with community leaders and social workers involved with the Somali community in Melbourne, there was much more of an immediate focus on the issue of clans, and they were described freely and voluntarily. One noted community leader described the clans as 'insurance' in case something goes wrong. He stressed the importance of the clan system in everyday life and described the way some elements of the clan protection system have been re-established in Australia through the organisations committed to Somali welfare.

It is important to note though, that despite the large number of Somali organisations (a fact that one community elder put down to clan pride and wishing to prove that one clan is as powerful as another by establishing clan-specific organisations), there are few, if any, questions about clan affiliation before joining. Indeed, I saw no evidence of any situation of clan-based discrimination within the Somali community in Melbourne.

Similarly, the sporting clubs organised by the young men remain a relatively clan-free arena. Spaaij argues that sport is seen as being inclusive and remains relatively free of clan politics. He also notes that within the Melbourne Giants Soccer club, although the founding members are Somali, and it is a Somali community organisation, there are players and spectators from other backgrounds such as Eritrea, Kenya, Sierra Leone and Ghana. There is a warm welcome for these other Africans to the club, based on their shared skin colour and common African identity (Spaaij 2012).

◊

All respondents spoke about the importance of Islam in their lives.

Many described Islam as a powerful force in their identity construction, and there was a lot of anxiety about how Islam is perceived by mainstream Australians, how the active practice of Islam is something that raises concerns in mainstream Australian society. One example was the way that hijab is perceived and reacted to. Within the Somali community in Melbourne, the vast majority of women are veiled and some of the respondents were frustrated that the veil is the only thing that people see about them, to the point that it negates other facets of their person.

Despite the challenges of participating fully in Islamic life while living in a Muslim minority country, the young people were proud of this particular aspect of their identities. This was not the case when asked about the importance of the Somali clan system. Some of the respondents acknowledged the purpose and use of the clan system in Somalia, but most were anxious to distance themselves from it in their lives in Australia. This was despite the fact that they were clearly well informed about the history of the clans and the way they operate both in Somalia and in Australia.

While the young people were reluctant to broach the topic of the clan system, they were very knowledgeable about it when it did arise. They gave examples of how membership of a particular clan had helped or hindered their family members in Somalia with business prospects and opportunities. They reflected on the role of the clans in Somalia and in Melbourne and there was a consensus that while the clans were an integral part of life in Somalia, they are no longer necessary for the younger generation living in Melbourne. None of the respondents identified themselves as belonging to a particular clan until asked directly. Islam was part of everyday practice, while clans existed for the young people in the abstract.

While the young people did not ascribe any importance to the clans in Australia, they thought the clan system was responsible for much of the bloodshed and conflict in Somalia; they also professed not to care very much about the clan system. However, it was clear that they had thought about it in quite some detail as they offered considered responses to all questions. This gave rise to the impression that these issues had been discussed before at length and indeed, discussions about the clans were usually lengthy without much prompting. This suggests that young Somalis actually do care about the clan system (and kinship more broadly) quite deeply despite their initial lack of interest in the topic.

5

Living under suspicion

It is particularly pertinent to note at this point that while sitting in front of an intelligent and articulate young adult (often the same age as myself), perhaps sharing some pastries and Lebanese coffee, or maybe talking in a brightly lit library or community centre, the ideas of suspicion and violence seemed awfully far away. When violence was raised by the young people, it was mostly in the context of the violence that occurred in Somalia. The topic often came up after a friendly rapport, and trust were established. However, there did not seem any discomfort when speaking about violence in Somalia. Indeed, details were relayed in a very pragmatic or practical tone, even when they concerned disturbing events recalled from childhood, or in some cases memories of traumatic injury or loss of loved ones.

> ***Sumaya**: Some areas are safer than others, but it's a scary place. I wouldn't go now. If someone gave me a ticket today I'd prefer to stay here. I remember I was 5 when we left. I remember Americans coming and storing all their weaponry in our household. I remember my brother got shot and all the blood everywhere. He was 15 and he was coming back from Qur'an school and he was on his way home and he got shot. And my brother brought him home covered in blood and then he went to hospital. The bullet had gone straight through so they stitched him up.*
>
> *Interview, 05.05.2013*

Some of the young generation had a strong grasp of recent Somali politics. It was clear that they discussed this with their peers and others within the community. It was culturally common to see men aged between 40 and 70 spend a full afternoon in a café with their friends in deep conversation. These conversations cover the situation in Somalia, Australian politics, the Somali community in Melbourne and other news and current affairs. The current affairs of Somalia are still quite present for the community in Melbourne, and it seems that some of the young people had heard and observed this and taken in some of that knowledge. So when describing the situation in Somalia, they were often very well informed.

On the other hand, there were some people who actively distanced themselves from Somalia, and professed disinterest about developments there. Indeed, responses regarding the cause of recent conflict were quite varied.

> ***Hani***: *My uncle always invites me [to Somalia] and I don't really want to go. I don't want to see a war-torn country. I don't know what I'd get out of it.*
>
> ***Sumaya***: *... it's not stable at all. The electricity still gets cut all the time and there are sometimes curfews and you can't go out.*
>
> *Focus group, 02.11.2012*
>
> ***Suleiman***: *I asked my mum when I was a young kid, a teenager, about why there was so much fighting in Somalia and she said there has always been fighting in Somalia and there always will be. That's why they had to leave.*
>
> *Interview, 20.02.2014*

Suleiman's answer is a very clear indication that in the mind of his mother, the fighting in Somalia is endemic, and will not change. He was not inclined to visit Somalia for this reason.

Cabaas was an example of an individual who took a great interest in Somalia. Consequently, he provided a nuanced answer, which displayed an understanding of Somali political history from the 1970s to the 1990s.

> ***Cabaas**: I think the war started because the president, Siyad Barre tried to do too much in our country too fast. He wanted to set up all this education stuff and to, you know, change the way people were living for years. Nobody likes to change so fast. And when the people were getting sick of him, other bad people stepped in and made things worse.*
>
> *Interview, 19.05.2013*

Scholars have noted the speed with which Siyad Barre made all references to clans a strictly punishable offence and outlawed traditional cultural practices, such as councils for resolving disputes, and even traditional ceremonies such as weddings. Once his regime was challenged, however, Barre sought to strengthen some clans at the cost of others in order to shore up his own rule (Hesse 2010, 251).

Aaliya describes the situation in Mogadishu in some detail.

> ***Aaliya**: I don't even know what to say about it [Mogadishu] anymore. There is so many wars I think from 1991 until today...so it's a really changed city. War after war after war. Many times people fled and then they came back and then another war broke out. The wars used to be between clans before and then it changed to some warlords fighting one another and then it changed to some kind of regions thing when other African troops intervened and then the war was between Somalis and outside troops and still that kind of war since 2006 is going on. There is an official government which was elected I think one month ago and people have good hopes but now the president he... nominated the prime minister I think it was the day before yesterday and people are really disappointed with the guy he came up because he is [a] business man and when the*

war was going on he was in Ethiopia and Kenya so he has really close ties with them and he doesn't know anything about politics is what some people say.

Interview, 01.06.2012

Aaliya describes the situation around the time of the Ethiopian military invasion of Somalia in 2006. This conflict was very prevalent in the minds of older Somalis, however it was not mentioned by any other of my younger respondents. The above account shows how much interest Aaliya takes in Somali political affairs. She engaged actively with family members in Somalia and studied politics in Australia. As the quotes below show, this was not the norm in the context of the interviews. Many more respondents claimed they had no idea about what happened in Somalia on a day-to-day basis.

***Mansuur**: I don't really care about it to be honest. It's not my home anymore.*

***Said**: No, I don't know a single thing about it. My life is in Melbourne.*

Focus group, 10.11.2012

There was a wide spectrum of responses on this topic. Some respondents regularly accessed news about Somalia, in Somali, Arabic and English. Others did not consider Somali current affairs to be important. Some of the respondents said that their parents had worked very hard to leave Somalia, that they wanted their children to be Australian and be informed about Australian issues. Others said that discussions about Somali politics were a source of distress within their homes and that their parents were unhappy speaking about the situation in Somalia as it was too upsetting for them.

Many of the young poeple mentioned accessing forums and chat rooms that discussed Somalia and aspects of Somali life. These online spaces were available to them to access privately, and not all had made their families aware of their participation in these forums or chats. These were a link for them to Somalia and a way of learning more about the situation there. They explained that it was good to have sources of information other than news broadcasts which they did not think were entirely trustworthy. In addition, the online spaces were populated with other young Somalis and they enjoyed conversing in Somali or English to learn more about developments in Somalia.

Aaliya's account below is a good indication of the range of conflicting interests vying for power in Somalia. According to her, after the overthrow of the Somali government, part of a conflict between the Darod and the Hawiye clan in which the Hawiye ousted the Darod, the conflict escalated. The Hawiye clan decide to 'eliminate' all members of the Darod clan or anybody with any connections (real or imaged). This has been likened to Rwandan genocide in 1994.

> ***Aaliya**: And after the war broke out my mum was of the clan who was persecuted because she was from the president's clan so she fled away from the city. My father's clan wasn't really that big, they didn't really have influence. It was just people sometimes they were accused like being part of the Darod clan because the bigger war was between the Darod and the Hawiye. The Darod was the clan that had the government, the Hawiye came, they overthrow the Darod and then they didn't overthrow only, they didn't go after the clan, you know the Sid clan of the president but they just started to eliminate anyone from the Darod clan like what happened with the Tutsi and Hutus in Rwanda. They said these people used to colonise us so everyone who looks like that clan, any connection, we just tell him: 'You are from that clan' and they kill him. So many of the Somali were persecuted for looking like that clan.*
>
> *Interview, 01.06.2012*

This account reveals the depth of confusion and the profound instability of the clans in Somalia at that time. Episodes of clan cleansing were carried out during the Somali civil war, and the testimony of survivors reveals that they were hunted down intentionally because of their group identity, sometimes by name by those who knew them (Kapteijns 2013, 14). Similar testimony was given by survivors of the Rwandan and Yugoslav genocides (Scheper-Hughes and Bourgois 2004). Sen's argument that conflict is engendered by the 'presumption that people can be uniquely categorized based on religion or culture' (Sen 2006, xv) is pertinent here. However, the clan cleansing took place between groups of people who shared religion and culture, despite belonging to different clans. This points to an oft-mentioned feature of the Somali conflict — the fragmented nature of the social and cultural landscape, despite ethnic and religious homogeneity.

There are many different versions of events that took place in Somalia during the 1990s. The clan warfare, although consistently reported on, has been difficult to document comprehensively and accurately. What is certain is that the Somali clans have at times been brutal in their eradication of each other's members. In times of such heightened conflict, as Aaliya described, it was not unusual to be misidentified as a member of a particular clan and injured or killed because of the assumed clan membership. Many respondents reported that their parents were able to identify clan membership of other Somalis by looking at them, which raises questions about the accuracy of such comments. It seems that mistakes were often made with regard to kinship in Somalia.

In discussion about violence in Somalia, many different theories were offered for the root cause of the continuing conflict. Suleiman's answer (above) as to the causes of violence in Somalia, reveals that in his family, at least, the violence is attributed to a personal characteristic of the Somalis. '*...she said there has always been fighting in Somalia and there always will be.*' Bilan agreed.

> ***Bilan***: *In Somalia when you're young, 8, 7, 9, 10, you must stand up for yourself, because you know children are really very cruel... but when you are older you should grow up from that culture, from that bullying culture. But the fighting continues with the Somalis. Especially between women. Once two people argue, it almost always ends up in fighting in Somalia, and bashing.*
>
> *Interview, 19.05.2013*

Her description of violence as a childhood last resort, is not unusual, but she believes that Somali children do not grow out of what she terms a 'bullying culture'. Here, Bilan implies that some Somalis remain childlike in their psychological development and are unable to grow up. She specifically notes that women are very likely to fight physically, which will be discussed in greater detail further on in this chapter. Aaliya also used the term 'bullying' to describe Somalis' violent responses:

> ***Aaliya***: *This is something that goes back a long time in Somali culture. Yes, I think it goes back because they fight about something so easy. Like 'you scratched my car'. And if you say 'what are you talking about, I didn't touch your car. Just get lost!' You say get lost and a fight starts. So, you know, the young Somali guys, do they hear that from their mothers? I don't know where they get it from. It's in their genes. ... You will hear some mums telling their boys 'you have to stand up for yourself and do whatever it takes'. And they wouldn't tell their children bullying is not acceptable in Australia. ... The Somalis are bullies... they really bully people.*
>
> *Interview, 01.06.2012*

Aaliya pointed out that the fighting culture 'goes back a long way' for Somalis and argued that it only takes something very small to set this off. She offers an explanation that this violence is genetic, however, she then reflects that this message is passed on from parents to children, and thus permeates from one generation to the next in a cultural sense, even in the Australian context, where she believes the acceptable culture is different from in Somalia. Interestingly, she states that the violence is passed from mother to son, indicating a belief that mothers are the parent most responsible for passing on cultural attributes and beliefs.

> ***Aaliya:*** *Also, Somali girls really fight. Australia doesn't know fighting, but in my country people fight.*
>
> ***Elizabeth**: Physically you mean?*
>
> ***Aaliya:*** *Yeah, it's normal. The Somalis are physical fighters. The women fight, especially the women fight too much. They fight about something which is really very easy like their kids, if one kid hits another child the mothers will be so furious. They will fight and the one who is defeated will go out and find her sisters and friends and whatever and bring a group and then this group they... bash each other.*
>
> *Interview, 01.06.2012*

Aaliya in particular, has a very strong opinion about Somali violence, and especially among women who she believes very easily resort to the use of physical violence as a response to their circumstances. She cites as an example a minor dispute which in her opinion will result in the use of physical violence. Again, she described a situation where there is a minor dispute. She argues that Somali women have as their first response to such situations, a violent instinct. They will not attempt to resolve the dispute through debate but will use physical strength to do so. She also describes how the situation will escalate from there, which includes seeking support from friends and family to gain the upper hand in a physical fight. While she was the most vocal about female violence, Aaliya was not the only person to describe women fighting in groups.

> ***Ishaar**: Women, they do the group fighting. It's something that existed... I don't know where it came from and we don't see it much as violent. Nobody sees it as violent. I guess this the way some women solve their problems together.*
>
> *Group interview 17.08.2014*

According to Ishaar, this physical violence is a dispute resolution system that is not perceived to be violent. This could be because it is common (although it was not mentioned by many of the young people), or because physical violence is not seen to be as serious if it occurs between women rather than men. According to Ishaar's explanation, this violence is not identified as such, perhaps because it is a customary way of resolving disputes.

> ***Absame:*** *I remember when we were in the camp in Kenya, there were so many women fighting all the time! We all lived very close together and they argued about their kids and their things (belongings). And I remember now, once I did see a big group of women doing a fight in the street. But my mum made us leave straight away.*
>
> *Focus group, 10.02.2014*

Absame's recollection does offer some support to the comments above about women fighting in groups; however the living conditions in refugee camps are are very stressful and fraught with uncertainty, and the situation he describes may be no more than a general response to these difficulties. Indeed, according to Absame's account, not all women participated in this fighting, with his mother at least choosing to remove herself and her children as quickly as she could.

Many of the respondents discussed the role of the clan system in the expressions of overt violence in Somalia.

> ***Bilan****: I think it's the clan system that's totally responsible for the war there. There are loads of other African countries where they're very poor too, and have the same droughts, and they're not fighting all the time.*
>
> *Interview, 19.05.2013*

Bilan was not one of the young people who was actively engaged in the discussion of Somali politics. However, she raises an important point in the comparison between Somalia and other countries which have similar climatic conditions. Her analysis suggests that drought and harsh environmental conditions are not the reasons for the conflict in Somalia.

The respondents did generally agree that the clan system played a role in the conflict. It was interesting that while the overwhelming response when asked for explanations of violence and conflict in Somalia referred directly to clans as an explanation, some young people were able to offer detailed insight, referring to specific historical events, particularly periods when different clans had political power. Other young people believed strongly that the clan system plays a big part in the creation and recreation of violence in Somalia but were not able to explain this in depth. Indeed, there was a sense from some respondents that the clan system itself is inherently violent, and that one shouldn't expect anything different from a group of people who subscribe to such a system.

Hani, for example, argued that the clan system is no more than a prejudice that is handed down from parents to their children. Her statement below supports the argument made by Aaliya earlier, that children absorb the beliefs and prejudices of their parents and act on them as well, although Hani believes that it is both mothers and fathers who transmit these messages.

> ***Hani**: And it's also the parents that influence the children — my father was completely against teaching about the tribes but there are parents who will tell the importance of their own tribe to their kids and that kid would go to school and find out a person from a different tribe and start that enmity and cause problems because that child is already thinking differently from a very young age. So that's what causes the problem. It's the parents that transfer that into their kids and their kids will do the same thing again.*
>
> *Interview, 20.01.2014*

Bilan contrasted the violence in Somalia with other more peaceful African countries, where she believes the environment is equally harsh. Suleiman makes reference to the harsh environment in Somalia as a reason for violence. Interestingly, however, there were no other reflections from the respondents on the severity of the climate and harsh living conditions in Somalia as a reason for violence to occur. This is in contrast to academic work and journalistic reportage where this idea is regularly raised as a possible reason for the extended conflict and violence in Somalia.

> ***Suleiman***: *I have heard that in the old days it was about making sure they could get enough water and grass for their camels. And I do believe that — it's always so dry there that people would die without getting access to water.*
>
> *Interview, 20.02.2014*

Some of the respondents who had shown that they were interested in Somali politics noted the outside interventions which they believed had exacerbated or prolonged the conflict.

> ***Aaliya***: *But before it used to be two men in Somalia they would have a physical fight and then they leave [finish the argument]. But now what happens in my country when two people argue, especially men, they use guns and kill each other ... now your enemy will kill you.*
>
> *Interview, 01.06.2012*
>
> ***Absame***: *It's a hard question. I don't know much about what is happening in Somalia today, but the way I understand it, there was a lot of involvements from America and the Soviets too. I want to know how all the guns and weapons got into there in the first place, because the Somalis couldn't afford all that steel and guns and tanks as well. I have discussed this a lot with my father and also with my friends.*
>
> *Group interview, 10.02.2014*

What came as a surprise in the data analysis, was the low correlation between discussions of violence with the young people, and the categories proliferated in the discourse. Part of the reason for this is likely to be that their life experience is quite different from those still living in Somalia, or those who have spent their adult life living there. Additionally, their conceptions and ideas of Somalia were quite different from those presented in academia and the media. This may be because they hear different recollections and interpretations from the older generations of Somalis in Melbourne.

One of the main features of overt violence is the ease with which it can be identified. The respondents were very free in their discussions of overt violence in Somalia and did not have any difficulty identifying such violence. Indeed, when asked about violence, they were able to talk about what had happened in Somalia in the past, and to provide some practical details. But there was a clear juncture in their minds between the violence that had taken place in Somalia and any overt violence that had been experienced in Australia. This is not to say that none of the respondents had ever experienced overt violence in Australia. However, overt violence that happened in Somalia belonged in Somalia, was explained in certain terms, and was removed from their life experience. Interestingly, while the young people discussed women fighting both in the refugee camps and in Australia as a way of resolving differences, they did not consider this to constitute violence. Rather, they thought of it as a perhaps regrettable but legitimate way of resolving differences.

In compiling this chapter, it became clear that the conversations with young people about overt violence in Somalia were one-on-one, rather than group discussions. That is, more people were talking about violence in Somalia when they were on their own. It appeared easier for individuals to discuss violence in Somalia in such a setting. This is perhaps because one of the features of the individual interviews is that they had a tendency to become more sombre and melancholy than the focus groups or group interviews. In a group situation, while sensitive topics were still able to be broached, there were often a multitude of opinions, so the same depth of individual experience was rarely traversed.

◊

This section now turns to describing covert violence as it has been experienced by the Somali community in Melbourne. This section is devoted mostly to my reflections on information I was given, and to situations described by people associated with the community (such as social workers, and community elders). While compiling this section on covert violence, it became clear that most of the evidence did not come from quotes from interviews and focus groups. Rather, the instances of covert violence presented below appeared in my field notes and observations of community meetings, and discussions with older Somalis in Melbourne.

One example of an issue which affected the Somali community deeply was the question of sending remittances to Somalia through official channels. Over the course of 2013 and 2014 it became more and more difficult for Somalis to send money back to their families using the Australian banking system. There was extended pressure on the banks to close the official money transfer channels due to suspicions that money entering Somalia was being diverted to support Al Shabaab. Numerous meetings about the situation were held in the Preston/West Heidelberg areas and in North Melbourne/Flemington. These meetings were both formal and informal, and some were just conversations between friends who were worried about the situation. They spoke about how it was nearly impossible to send money through any of the big four banks and the smaller credit unions were also steadily closing their remittance programs.

Community sentiment was that there were two levels of obstacles to those wishing to send money to Somalia. Firstly, there was an official level, which comprised the banks and credit unions closing off the flow of money to Somalia. Secondly, and more difficult, were the personal obstacles encountered depending on which person was serving at a particular bank. There were theories about the best time to go to a bank, and which sort of person should go (old, young, male, female) to have the best chance of transferring money.

At one meeting, there was an extended discussion about remittances and the increasing difficulty encountered when sending money home. Some people told stories about how going to a particular bank at different times of day, or on different days would make the process easier or more difficult depending on who was serving behind the counter. There was agreement that sending money to Somalia was regarded with deep suspicion by many bank employees.

Westpac was the last Australian bank allowing remittances to be sent to Somalia. This avenue was finally closed after much uncertainty on March 31, 2015 (Cummings 4 April 2015), putting already vulnerable individuals in Somalia at further risk (Oxfam Australia Media 30 March 2015). This caused a great deal of stress and worry to some community members in Melbourne, although they did acknowledge the risk that once they sent money to Somalia they did not have control over it, and they believed there was a significant chance that the money could be intercepted (some told stories of sending money which never arrived).

This is a fitting example of how covert violence operates. There is inherent violence in stopping a flow of money to a vulnerable population, especially when it is known how much this population relies on remittances from outside their country (although the data is inexact, it is commly estimated that between 25 - 40% of Somalia's GDP comprises of remittances. The priority is to ensure that

Al Shabaab has a reduced chance of getting funds from outside Somalia, (Cummings 4 April 2015). In order to ensure this, the money flow is suspended to innocent people who may need financial aid desperately. Indeed, the decision to stop the flow of remittances is an example of 'legally allowable activities that disrupt or influence the democratic flow of civil life in favour of "higher powers" and against the well-being or rights of citizens or workers', which can be understood as a form of covert violence. This decision 'selectively victimizes certain members of the population' (Colaguori 2010, 398).

The personal obstacles encountered are also examples of covert violence, although this is not officially sanctioned in the same way. The community members pointed out that they were at the mercy of different bank tellers and that they believed that their ethnicity and the destination they wished to send their money to were regarded with mistrust. According to their reports, sometimes they were able to send money, and other times the same bank branch would refuse with no reason given. In this case, they felt that the bank employees had control over whether their money was sent to Somalia or not. They altered their routines, behaviour and 'cover stories' about what the money was needed for in Somalia in order to have the best chance of sending money back to Somalia.

As mentioned above, the majority of fieldwork data in this section came from participant observation, rather than from conversations with Gen 1.5. The issue of remittances shows this clearly, because in my conversations with the young people, while there was an awareness of the money being sent back to Somalia, it became clear that Gen 1.5 were not expected to make contributions to funds, and they had a limited engagement with the issue.

◊

In conceiving of covert violence, the disadvantage that Somalis face in their capacity as recently arrived refugees featured strongly. In order to gain a clearer understanding of the way that Somalis access social services, social workers who had years of experience working with the Somali Australian community were also interviewed. They spoke at length about how recent cuts to the sector had forced agencies to reduce their case load numbers. One social worker said that the first clients to be removed from the active case lists were Somalis. This was because the agency had tightened its criteria for accepting clients, and their reasoning was that, based on experience, the Somali clients chose to access support networks within their own communities much more often than other minority groups and were therefore more likely to resolve their issues without the support of the agency. In her words,

> ***Social Worker:*** *Somalis are known for sorting their own problems out. They sometimes take advantage of the services we offer, but just as often, I think, I will work with a client and come up with a plan to deal with some issue. And I mean work over an extended period of time, say 12 weeks. And then they don't bother coming one week, and I hear through the grapevine that they have moved away from their particular problem, to another suburb or state, or that they have been given a job by a relative, or invited to live in another family's house. So my work is wasted. They just, you know, they keep their problems 'in-house'.*
>
> *Interview, 08.12.2014*

The use of the word 'wasted' above suggests annoyance on the part of the social worker. It also suggests that she feels her work has no impact beyond the immediate situation. Perhaps she considers her contribution less as an educative process, and more as a means to an end in an immediate crisis situation.

This is undoubtedly a difficult situation, and the response of the agency is not unreasonable. It is a sad fact that when funds are cut to service areas, the service providers must tighten the criteria by which they accept applications for assistance. However, this situation is likely also indicative of everyday misunderstandings between the Australian concept of providing assistance and the Somali method of solving problems. One recurrent theme in the discussion with Somalis of all ages, was the benefit of being be able to rely on your family (and sometimes your clan) in order to solve personal problems. Indeed, this reliance on extended networks can be seen as a form of social capital in the Bourdieuian sense. This is particularly true because the power that accrues through one network of belonging is at the expense of another. That is, Somalis who take advantage of their kinship and clan networks cut themselves off from the local Australian systems in place to offer assistance in times of need. This is further evidence of the strategy of looking inwards and choosing to rely on resources from within the community.

There are some exceptions. The following is an example of a formalised aid agreement between a Somali community organisation and the Sherriff's office for the resolution of traffic infringements (of which there are apparently many, because many Somalis drive taxis for a living). The president of this well-respected community organisation described a situation as follows:

> ***President***: *Imagine you have a Somali taxi driver who is 45 or 50. He runs through a red light or gets a parking ticket and is sent an infringement notice in the mail. He receives the official envelope and he is too scared to open it, so he puts it away in a drawer and forgets about it. Or maybe he does open it, but he is not able to understand the official language that is printed there. So he puts it away and tries to forget about it. Then a couple of months later, another letter arrives from the same place. He knows that there is bad news, but he tries to ignore it again. Then again, another letter arrives and when he opens this he sees that now he has to pay three fines instead of just one, or maybe he has to go to court.*

His English skills are not very good, and he is very worried about the police involvement. So he might come to us for help and show us all his letters. And always we say, 'why didn't you come earlier? We could have solved this problem much faster'.

Interview, 13.11.2012

The arrangement with the Sherriff's office allows the taxi driver (or another individual in a similar situation) to convert some of his fines to community service, and to carry out the community service in an organisation that is linked to the local Somali community.

The above shows an example of successful 'in-house' management of problems, however, there were also multiple issues identified as being very difficult for the community to manage 'in-house'. Youth unemployment is a significant problem for Somali males, according to Iman, a young social worker who is engaged professionally with Somali young men. According to him Somali male high school dropouts are overrepresented in comparison to their peers. He argued that because Somali parents do not enforce discipline in the home for their sons, they may not gain employment for many years. This unemployment can cause familial discord, including parental nagging and sibling jealousy. However, he agreed that the Somali community prefers to manage these cases independently, without seeking help from the community services that exist to address these problems in the mainstream community as well as for minority groups.

According to Iman, it would be useful for young Somali men to engage with the social services that are available.

***Iman**: I try to talk to these guys, you know, to tell them that there is nothing embarrassing about seeing a social worker. It might really improve their life! But they just won't do it. They prefer to ignore their problems. It is difficult for them to talk to an outsider about what is going on in their life, and I think they feel afraid to show* *that they are weak.*

Interview, 13.02.2014

When asked about accessing financial help from Centrelink, Iman said that some of his clients 'couldn't face' going into a Centrelink office. Pressed for further details, he responded that in his opinion, Centrelink makes it difficult for people to access payments to save money.

> ***Iman**: But they do that for everyone, not just the Somalis. No one likes to fill out the forms, and take in the ID, and wait and wait and wait. But you just have to do it.*
>
> *Interview, 13.02.2014*

While this could be argued to be a form of covert violence (although, it could perhaps more convincingly be described as poor bureaucratic practice), Iman does not believe that it is targeted at Somalis. Nevertheless, he agreed that it is difficult to convince Somalis to access social services. It is worth noting here though, that if young Somalis know that they are able to rely on family networks for help, they may consider accessing social services a waste of time. However, it is also important to remember that the relatively recent arrival of large numbers of Somalis to Melbourne, coupled with their status as refugees has had an effect on the ability they have to mobilise resources and support members of their community. Viewed in this way, the community tendency to look inward for help and support, may have adverse effects.

Iman told me that he was part of a team seeking to address young Somali men's reluctance to present at medical centres when ill. According to Iman, it is difficult to persuade young Somali men to go to medical centres, both when they are ill and as a preventative measure or for regular check-ups. Previous studies have shown that Somali women are confused by the western model of medical care

(Pavlish, Noor, and Brandt 2010), and that Somalis often present to an Emergency department rather than attending a medical clinic for relatively minor illnesses (DeShaw August 2006).

Some of the respondents said that there is confusion about whether they will need to pay for medical care at a clinic. There are difficulties understanding which clinics bulk bill, and for what services, so the fear of being charged for medical attention causes them not to present at all. This could be interpreted as a form of covert violence, because although the medical centres are there and available for all patients, a portion of the patients does not have the education or understanding of the local bureaucracy to take advantage of the services available to them. This is an example of low social capital impacting access to social services, and potentially resulting in poor health outcomes that could have been prevented.

◊

Covert violence is difficult to pin down because it has been absorbed 'like air' and is very difficult to escape from (Eagleton and Bourdieu 1992). In the cases above, which can be taken as emblematic of many similar situations in the Somali community in Melbourne, we can see the latent power structures which have imposed hierarchies and 'ways of being and knowing the world that unevenly distribute suffering, and limit even the ways in which we can imagine the possibility of an alternative world' (Schubert 2008, 192). The over-representation of Africans (and other minority groups) in crime statistics in Australia (Centre for Multicultural Youth 2014) can be thought of in terms of covert violence. The structural violence of discrimination against ethnic minorities by local legal systems and the media is well documented (Roulstone and Mason-Bish 2013; Alia and Bull 2005). In the above case of the taxi driver, the structural violence rests at a deeper level because it has led to a situation where an individual is being penalised for their lack of understanding of the local legal system — another reflection of the lack of social capital among the Somali community. However, the remedial system they have organised highlights how strong and capable the Somali community can be, despite their disadvantage.

Power is expressed through multiple layers of relations and can be expressed in seemingly hidden forms. One issue which arose on a regular basis was the Somalis' mistrust of official and bureaucratic processes. This included fear of the police, as has been reported in the context of African youths (and other ethnic minority groups) (Wilson 2007; Milovanovic 16 March 2010; Murphy 2011). This mistrust can result in further disadvantage to the Somali community in the following way.

A number of Somali community workers and a social worker told of their belief that the number of Somalis as stated in the census is incorrect. They said that many Somalis are afraid to admit their ethnicity on the census form. They are also afraid to give their religion as Islam, so they leave the section blank, or they claim to speak English at home. According to community service workers, this is a problem because funding and services are targeted at areas where there is the highest need, and if the census data shows fewer numbers of Somalis residing in a certain area, funding and services may be reduced in that area.

According to the social workers, the fear that causes Somali Australians to either lie or refuse to answer questions about their ethnicity, religion and culture leads directly to negative consequences for them (in this case, funding cuts to services they might need to access). This is an example of structural violence reproducing the conditions which allow it to flourish, as it leads to a cycle of further disadvantage for Somalis in Melbourne.

◊

This section focuses on the responses of the participants and their reflections on the perception and representations of Somalis as violent. There are many examples of covert violence, accompanied by their reflections. These examples reflect the lived experience of Gen 1.5. For instance, the following quote is a reconstruction of a conversation with a young man who did not want to be recorded.

> ***Elizabeth**: What can you tell me about violence in the Somali community in Melbourne?*
>
> ***X**: I don't want to talk about this issue, because it gets taken out of context and looks very bad for us, for my community.*
>
> ***Elizabeth**: Can you explain a bit more what you mean?*
>
> ***X**: I don't want to say anything about it because, even if we do have some violence problems in our people in Melbourne, I don't think it's right to focus on that. Every group of people has some problems, even if they're rich and white. I think that when we talk about it all the time, we are making sure that that's the thing that people remember about us.*
>
> *Interview, 09.08.2014*

The conversation continued in a similar vein for a few moments, probing gently into why this young man did not want to engage with the issue of violence in the Somali community. He believes that there is violence in every group of people because there are good and bad people everywhere. In response to his distress, the conversation turned to other topics. His sense of unease was very strong, a reminder that this is a significant personal issue for some young Somalis.

One fascinating insight came in discussing violence in the Somali community in Melbourne with young women who immediately assumed that this was referring to domestic violence. The men, on the other hand, thought first of criminal violence and assaults. See the two contrasting responses below:

> ***Elizabeth**: What do you think about violence in the Somali community?*
>
> ***Ismahaan**: If that happens, if a woman gets bashed, she will retaliate and get her husband back.*
>
> *Interview, 04.05.2013*
>
> ***Elizabeth**: What do you think about violence in the Somali community?*
>
> **Iman**: *I think there are some problems with the police, yes.*
>
> *Interview, 13.02.2014*

This reveals much about what the females and males consider violent, and what features in their daily lives constitute violence. Violence is often described as a masculine trait, and it is true that violent crime occurs much more among males than females (Ray 2011, 83), but the female respondents described incidents of female violence towards males in retaliation to intimate partner violence (this violence would almost certainly go unreported). The women used language such as a man being 'taught a lesson' by his wife (and in some cases her sisters, cousins, and friends, which adds an interesting dimension to the conversation about women's group violence above). Interestingly, none of the males had any such experiences to relate. According to the women, this was most likely due to the need for men to save face and not appear weak or emasculated. The women stressed that because divorce was a frequent and accepted feature of Somali culture (both in Somalia and in Melbourne), there was recourse for women if they suffered at the hands of their husbands and also a way out of a violent marriage. However, this could also be an indication that the men did not consider that such interactions constituted violence.

> ***Layla***: *I had a cousin that was suffering very badly from her husband. She didn't want to break up the marriage because it had been a long time to organise it with all her family. But this guy lost his job and he was at home all the time, the whole day, and he was giving her trouble. And she couldn't take it any more. She spoke to his parents and they went to the Imam and she got a divorce a year after they got married. I think she felt guilty because her parents paid for them to go do it in Somalia. But you can't stay in a relationship where there is violence!*
>
> ***Nafiso***: *I never knew anyone in a violent marriage, but I heard some stories about a guy who was bashing his wife, and she got all her sisters to go round there and they pulled his hair and they taught him a lesson. And he stopped doing it.*
>
> *Focus group, 15.01.2014*

The above reflections indicate that the women in both cases 'found a solution' to the problem of violence in their marriage. One solution was to leave the marriage, the other solution was to intimidate the violent partner into stopping his previous behaviour. In the discussion in this particular focus group the respondents did not judge that one solution was better than another. Rather, they were pleased that the women involved had been able to solve their problems with their husbands.

The young men chose to tell stories of friends and acquaintances who had been involved with the police (all felt that this involvement was unfair). There is a significant body of work that deals with youth and police relations, particularly ethnic minority youth. Studies have suggested that minority youth have a more troubled relationship with police and report more personal negative experience with police officers (Brunson and Weitzer 2009).

It has also been well documented that police have a tendency to mistrust young black males (Piliavin and Briar 1964; Black and Reiss 1970; Hurst, Frank, and Browning 2000). More recently, scholarly work has been devoted to examining the complex ways citizens manage their behaviour towards the police (Weitzer and Brunson 2009). Discussing minority male relationships with police, Robin Engel suggests that the wider the gap in the social background of the police officers and the minority youth, the more likely mutual displays of disrespect are. Engel states 'it is possible that particular types of citizens (e.g., young minority males) may act in disrespectful or otherwise resistant ways to symbolize their perceptions of injustice' (Engel 2003, 477).

In my interview with one of the young men who did not wish to be recorded, he explained that the police expect Somalis to be criminals, so what is the point of telling them otherwise?

> ***X**: They're always on the lookout for us. Especially if we're in a group of friends together. Sometimes I wonder if we should do something bad just to see what happens. I know they're going to question us anyway, so maybe we should make it worth the hassle?*
>
> *Interview, 09.08.2014*

The above is a reconstructed quote, and the conversation continued for some time with me trying to unpack the statement '*I know they're going to question us anyway, so maybe we should make it worth the hassle?*'. Essentially, this young man believed that he would be targeted because of his ethnicity and that this would probably result in negative consequences for him, regardless of his innocence or guilt. He said he was sometimes tempted to 'play up' to this increased police attention because then at least he would 'deserve' the attention. However, his friends had always talked him out of such behaviour, warning that the result would be damaging for him and his family.

The idea that young Somalis are unfairly targeted by police was very common with the respondents.

> ***Bashir****: There is always, always, always someone from our community in trouble with the police. It's obvious it's because we are Somali*
>
> ***Bilan****: It's still hard because, we're not trained to trust the police, you know? The boys expect bad things will happen if they go there, and sometimes I think that's probably true.*
>
> *Focus group, 02.11.2012*

When pressed about what she meant by 'not trained to trust the police', Bilan explained that law enforcement was something to be feared in Somalia, and that many parents of young people had a visible attitude of mistrust.

> ***Bilan****: Our parents are afraid of the police. I knew that even from a very young age. They would cross over the street to avoid them, and you could tell that they were very nervous.*
>
> *Interview, 19.05.2013*

Bilan's parents' behaviour served to reinforce the way that power is expressed in society through multiple layers of relations. People are always conceiving of themselves in terms of the categories available to them. Bilan's parents consider themselves as untrustworthy in the eyes of the police or believe that police are suspicious of them because they are seen as very dangerous. This move encourages Bilan to ask herself whether she needs to be wary of police as well, even in Australia. Gen 1.5 Somalis in Melbourne grow up in a space where they are forced to view themselves in terms of the constructed categories prevalent, and to negotiate their identity formation and expression against the backdrop of embedded power relations in society. On a practical level, this is also simply due to the fact that police in Somalia operate in a very different way compared with police in Melbourne. In Somalia, police and other official representatives were certainly people to be feared, rather than trusted.

However, this is not to suggest that young Somali Australians do not have grounds for fearing members of the police force in Australia. There have long been questions about how the police interact with young African Australian males in particular. In 2013, a case brought against Victoria Police by six young African Australian men was settled outside court the day before it was due to be heard. The young men accused Victoria Police of widespread racial profiling and alleged that police force members were stopping them for unwarranted searching and questioning. As part of the case, they requested a statistician, Professor Ian Gordon, to analyse police notes. He found that young African Australian men living in Flemington and North Melbourne were stopped two and a half times more often than their counterparts who were not of African descent (Donovan 2013).

Police diary notes which were to be used as evidence in the case showed that police had described African Australian males as 'criminals loitering in the area'. 'Unable to provide police with reason of why they were there or what they were doing. Nervous in police presence' was an example given by police in a stop where they required an African Australian teenager to justify being in a public place. The law requires police to have a legitimate reason to interfere with a person's freedom of movement (Seidel and Hopkins 2013). Additionally, Professor Gordon's analysis of police statistics found that in fact young men of African descent committed significantly less crime than other populations in Flemington and North Melbourne (Donovan 2013).

In 2015, two of the men who brought the original case against Victoria Police released a report titled *The More Things Change, The More They Stay the Same*. Daniel Haile-Michael and Maki Issa spoke with young people in Sunshine, Flemington, Noble Park and Dandenong about their experiences with the police and found that negative experiences were still common, public occurrences which caused isolation, fear and anxiety (Haile-Michael and Issa 2015).

It seems that young Somali Australians consistently see themselves as the type of people who will be targeted by police and are likely to end up in jail. An example of tension was observed between a group of Somali young men and police officers at Footscray train station in Melbourne's west in September 2013. At that time construction works were being undertaken at the footbridge, with some ramps and stairs blocked off. There was a group of around eight young men, aged between 17 and 25 or so. They were in high spirits; laughing and talking and pushing each other around teasingly. Two uniformed police officers, one male and one female were approaching along the footpath. They were heading in the direction of the group of boys, but it was not clear if they intended to speak with them or not. As soon as they were noticed, the laughter died away. The group dispersed immediately, in groups of twos and threes. Some went into the station, others walked away in the same direction the police officers were heading, and two even crossed the road against the lights to avoid having to speak with them.

I was with a friend — a young Somali woman, active in the community, who told me that this is not uncommon. I was amazed that it was preferable to jay-walk in front of police officers rather than be found in a seemingly innocent group of friends, however she said that in the minds of young Somali men, anything is better than having contact with a police officer. After all, once they are across the road, they can always run away if necessary. Recounting this incident to some of the respondents, their response was matter-of-fact. Many believed it is better to disappear rather than risk a confrontation. They thought similarly about ticket inspectors on public transport. Having watched young Somalis exit a train as ticket inspectors boarded it, or pass through to the next carriage in an attempt to exit successfully at the next stop, I had always assumed that they had not had a valid ticket. Perhaps this is not always the case.

Iman explained that in his work as a social worker he had dealt with many young men who felt they were targeted unfairly by the police.

> ***Iman***: *I talk to heaps of these guys, you know? They feel like they're trying to live their life and when they hang out in the mall, or go out with their friends, there's always someone watching them and the police get involved if there's a big group of them.*
>
> *Interview, 27.04.2014*

Absame reflects that part of the problem for the Somali youth comes down to a lack of understanding of the law and of Australia's bureaucratic processes and of their parents' to link to a network that would be able to help their sons (lawyers, social workers, medical officers for example).

> ***Absame***: *Some of the young guys act violent and sometimes he have problems with maybe the ticket inspectors and sometimes he acted like... we accused him of acting like he was above the law: driving without license, you know things like normal teenagers do. I hear from other people — there's too many young Somalis who are in jail. They are in jail for some easy things which if they have some people to fix, or if their parents know more about the law or if their parents could help them... It's a very, very big disadvantage.*
>
> ***Elizabeth***: *So you think if they had better representation they wouldn't be in jail...*
>
> ***Absame***: *Better representation, yeah, because they often go to jail, for things that young Australian people — teenagers wouldn't go to jail for.*
>
> *Focus group, 10.02.2014*

These Somali youth are exposed to a form of inherent structural violence. Poor representation and understanding of the structures of the legal system, for instance, can lead to an inflated proportion of Somalis appearing in crime statistics. This, in turn, may reinforce notions of inherent violence in Somalis and reproduces the conditions for a cyclic reproduction of events (Nolan et al. 2014, 19-20). Additionally, there have been incidents of police and journalists analysing statistics incorrectly and producing data which inaccurately claims that young Somali Australians and African Australians more generally commit more crimes than other populations. It is difficult to overstate the implications of this inaccuracy, both in terms of the effect it has on the young people themselves, and in terms of the way it encourages others to view them in a certain way. The reinforcement of such inaccuracies entrenches ideological categories and reinforces what are, for Gen 1.5, prejudiced distributions of power.

Many of the young people talked about how crime was a reality for anyone living in any country in the world and the way that if a Muslim commits a crime, the lead story is their identification as Muslim and how that must have contributed to the crime.

> ***Omar***: *I read an article a couple of years ago on the Herald Sun, and it was two young men that I actually knew they were Ethiopian. They were non-Muslim. And they got intoxicated and they were harassing people, I can't remember exactly what the article was on. But they got categorised as young Muslim youth who weren't used to this culture, and alcohol and the lifestyle. But there was actually a lot of alcohol back in Ethiopia and even in Somalia... there was alcohol back home. It's not something new but they were getting categorised as Muslims who never drank alcohol in their life, but now that they're here they get introduced to alcohol, they don't know how to handle it. So I was like, 'Yeah, I recognise these guys and they're not Muslim, so you can't say there's no alcohol in their culture'.*
>
> *Group interview, 11.05.2014*

Here, Omar is referring to a situation where Islam was used directly as an explanation for antisocial behaviour. The assumption that the young men were Muslim, and this explained their unfamiliarity with alcohol carries two levels of falsity. In the first, explicit level, the reportage was incorrect about the Muslim origins of the youths. In the second instance, although alcohol is not tolerated by Islam, many young people said that there was alcohol in Somalia (where the population is almost universally Muslim).

This kind of reportage seems at first glance to be a reasonable and even sympathetic account of events. However, making such essentialist statements about Islam and what is permitted for Muslims homogenises them, and reduces their agency. It encourages us to think of Muslims as a mass of people who are bound tightly by Islam and never experiment or do anything that falls outside a literal interpretation of the religion. Such statements would not likely be made about Christians for example — indeed it is unlikely that any newspaper would claim no Christians have tattoos, even though the bible expressly forbids it.

One common reflection by the young people was on the loss of fathers during violent conflict or in circumstances unknown.

> ***Amal**: The high school I went to [in Australia], many of the Somali students there didn't have fathers. Some of them said their father left in the morning and never came back. They couldn't bury them ... 80% of them. They shot Meriam's dad right in front of the family...*
>
> *Interview, 21.01.2014*

They worried about the effects of this loss, both on their mothers and on the children, raised fatherless in Australia. This was also an area of concern for the older women who claimed that the lack of a father can lead to young men in particular 'getting into trouble with the law'. The problem of absent or disengaged fathers has also been remarked on in other studies with some young Somalis in

London explaining that absent fathers are part of the reason Somali boys get into criminal activity, because of lack of authority and discipline (Harding, Clarke, and Chappell 2007, 15). In 2009, Farah Aw-Osman, the president of Canadian Friends of Somalia wrote an essay pointing to the problem of absent fathers as directly linked to crime rates among Somali youth in Ottawa, saying: 'The absence of Somali fathers in the lives of their children is a key reason as to why so many youth have fallen into the hands of the criminal justice system' (Aw-Ossman 2009). Some of the young people agreed:

> ***Elizabeth***: *So who is responsible for this situation?*
>
> ***Ismahaan***: *Well in the families it's just like they're single mothers. The fathers are really useless, the African fathers, especially the Somali fathers are really... not involved.*
>
> ***Elizabeth***: *Do you mean here, in Melbourne? Or also in Somalia?*
>
> ***Ismahaan***: *Even in Somalia. After the war they lost their responsibility. But in Somalia you can give them some concession why this happened because there is no work, there is nothing to work for so they turn to chewing qat. You know what qat is? Some kind of drug whatever it is and the mothers are, especially in Somali society, the mothers took the role of father, of bringing money to the family and the role of mother as well. But in Australia... I don't know, they really, really don't know. They [the men] lost the responsibility of being a father, of being role models to their children. Some of them even doesn't know which school their children is studying at.*
>
> *Interview, 03.12.2014*

Many of the respondents identified a change in gender roles upon arrival to Australia, with the mothers taking on more responsibility inside and outside the household. This is discussed further in the following chapters. Suffice to say, the lack of strong discipline from fathers was a recurrent theme in discussing many of the issues faced by Somali young men in Melbourne. It is worth mentioning here that in discussion with older women (the first-generation migrants), many expressed serious concerns for their sons' futures. They were worried about employment, their attendance at university, or other study (including apprenticeships). There was a sense that the world is more difficult to navigate for males than females. When asked why, a common response was that women can simply manage more things in life. One mother said 'things come easier for my daughters'. Another said there are 'too many distractions for the boys'. Certainly, the mothers had a gendered view of their children's capability.

◊

When reading ethnographic and anthropological accounts of violence, there is often a visceral nature to the retelling. There are details (such as the use of bamboo poles to impale victims during the massacres in Rwanda (Gourevitch 2004), or the physical torture carried out in Cambodia in the killing fields (Laban Hinton 2004). The respondents did not tell me any raw details. They didn't seem to know the details of physical violence that had been perpetrated in Somalia. They spoke at length of political conflict, food scarcity, and the continual disruptions of living in a war-torn country (the unreliability of the electricity supply, the lack of petrol, the sirens and raids which meant they had to hide). From my interaction with older Somali women, it seems the first generation migrants have not told their children many details. In discussions with the mothers, when asked about their choice to speak with their children about what it was like in Somalia before and during the civil war, their responses indicated that they did not wish to burden their children with this knowledge.

> ***Mother 1:*** *Why [would] I tell my children this? It was a very bad time. They do not want to remember these things.*
>
> ***Mother 2:*** *We start a new life in Australia. It was difficult to get here, and now we have a different future. I do not want my children*

> *to have this heavy past with them all the time.*
>
> *Focus group, 30.03.2014*

Das and Kleinman describe how the recovery of the 'everyday' requires a renewed capability to address the future.

> How does one shape a future in which the collective experience of violence and terror can find recognition in the narratives of larger entities such as the nation and the state? And at the level of interpersonal relations, how does one contain and seal off the violence that might poison the life of future generations? (Das and Kleinman 2011, 4)

One possible conclusion here is that Somali first generation migrants to Australia have made strong efforts to contain and seal off the violence they suffered. This is manifest in many ways. It seems that the older generation has made a conscious choice to withhold certain information from their children. The respondents told me that their parents wanted to ensure they grew up with the knowledge that when Somalia was in a peaceful period, it was a beautiful country, and the good memories they have of the parks, universities and city life.

> ***Sumaya**: Our parents have such amazing love for the country because it's their home... So they have these beautiful memories. Whereas, all our memories are of trouble and war. To them, they remember the days when there was university, cafes, and beaches. It was beautiful! I wish I could go to that Somalia. The photos are so nice to look at. To be forced out and to see the country destroyed.... It's still their home because they came here as adults. But to us, it's not home, because we were raised here and it's normal for us. So I really feel that I belong here.*
>
> *Interview, 05.05.2013*

◊

A final important idea to cover in this chapter is that of 'radicalisation'. When presenting the examples of violent acts perpetrated by Somalis, the notion of Gen 1.5 becoming radicalised was briefly discussed. This term is often used in connection with an individual who has been exposed to extremist views, before taking these views on. Such individuals are considered to be willing to deploy extreme acts to promote their views; often deemed to be acts of terrorism.

None of the young people volunteered the term 'radicalisation' during the interviews and focus groups without me introducing it into conversation. It is interesting that the term which is so often used by academics, reporters, authority figures and members of government was not in the lexicon of the Gen 1.5ers. However, many wished to discuss events such as terror raids in Melbourne in September 2012 and August 2013 and reports that *dugsis* (cultural schools, which are similar to Sunday School, but also include elements of education such as Arabic grammar and letter formation) may be teaching extremist doctrines. They were also worried by reports that groups such as Al Shabaab are recruiting young men to fight jihad. Interestingly, the media reports they mentioned very rarely linked *dugsis* directly with terror attacks. In fact, some of the reports were about the calls from within the Somali community to regulate *dugsis* in Melbourne (Aly 2013; Shand 2013).

The collective memory of the young people regarding media reports of *dugsis* teaching terrorism was not supported by the evidence found. Indeed, it has been suggested that scholars are insufficiently critical of the construction of collective memories (Maynes, Pierce, and Laslett 2008, 62). Beth Roy has also shown how strong emotions and political motivations can alter and reconstruct memory (Roy 1999). The young people clearly had strong feelings about their representation in the media, and it is possible that this coloured their memory, and led to what Luisa Passerini describes as 'distortions or "false memory"' (Passerini 2005, 4).

In general, there was a strong sense of injustice around these events and reporting, and in some focus groups I had to call for quiet more than once to allow everyone's ideas to be heard.

> ***Hani**: I was overseas when this news happened in Australia, and I came back and heard it and I was gobsmacked. I was like, 'Seriously? Kids learning Qur'an leads to terrorism?' I found that to be the most stupid thing...the most stupid reporting. If they actually came in and saw what the kids were learning, they would never conclude to that. Never!*
>
> ***Ismahaan**: I think everyone had the same feeling of 'Oh my God, you're kidding me'. Just disbelief. It was ridiculous.*
>
> ***Amal**: And come on! We're the ones doing the teaching! It's not some guy who has come from Somalia. It's us! We grew up here. When I saw the reports on TV I couldn't understand it, it was all foreign to me. And it's really strange to see it on TV and think 'Oh, that's what people think of me'.*
>
> *Focus group, 02.11.2012*

The above exchange illustrates the shock felt by the young people and the distance they place between their practicing of Islam and the way it has been interpreted. Nobody in any focus groups or interviews discussed radicalisation as a real threat from the Somali community. Some young people wanted to explain that they believe that the threat in general has been grossly overestimated.

> ***Hani**: My brother, one of them, he started to practice at 19 or 20, and to other people, as soon as a boy starts to practice his religion, even though it's a private thing, it's like what's happening? Is he going to be an extremist? Should we be worried? He lost some friends for sure when he became religious. I think girls have*

> *more permission to practice their religion. And for my brother, it didn't have anything to do with that kind of radicalisation. He never thought of going overseas and getting into war. He just wanted to better himself. He would just do little things that the prophet would teach us in our books, little good things like charity and good deeds. And he became a better person; he was a positive person, a much happier person than before. And my whole family were really happy.*
>
> *Interview, 20.12.2014*

Hani's response indicates that for some of her brother's friends, his decision to start practicing his faith was unacceptable. I asked Hani about what she meant by 'started to practice'. She explained that while her brother had attended mosque and religious events with the family (he still lived at home), he had not read Qur'an or prayed daily. He made a decision to start doing these things, and also (she suspects) to stop drinking alcohol with his non-Muslim friends when they were out.

> ***Kadiye***: *I never knew anyone who was approached to go and fight, or to do any terror acts.*
>
> ***Said***: *There is always somebody saying that we can't be trusted and that we will fight for the terrorist cause, but I don't meet anyone who actually feels this way. Sure, we think what is happening in Somalia is very bad news. But our home is here now, and we are not going to risk everything our parents have done for us to go to a war that doesn't belong to us.*
>
> *Focus group, 10.11.2012*

Said was not unusual in mentioning a sense of responsibility towards his parents and the sacrifices they have made. Again, Said speaks about belonging here — and he uses his allegiance to Australia to explain why he would not go to a war that does not belong to him.

There was another answer which came up over the course of the interviews and the discussion groups which was surprising.

> ***Naado***: *And it's just another hit, another jab, you know? Now they say the Somali community teaches terrorism at school and tries to influence children. It's basically like the bogey-man. They make it bigger and bigger every time they do reportage.*
>
> ***Kadiye***: *People, you know, they got to be scared of something. So maybe it just has to be us?*
>
> ***Cabass:*** *Every time I'm watching like a detective show or something and the bad guy is Muslim — he's always Muslim! I think about how it's shown as good guys versus bad guys. And if you want to be a good guy, then you have to have a bad guy to fight against.*
>
> *Focus group, 10.11.2012*

These comments display a belief in the human need to categorise and label others. The young people reflected on their personal experience and the broader context of terrorism and fear of the other. They worried that the media fuelled fear, with little or no evidence to back the claims up.

When I asked them what they thought about second-generation terrorism (explaining that it means acts of terrorism carried out by people who were born or raised in the country they commit the attacks in), they dismissed the phenomenon altogether.

> ***Amal***: *I have heard about that, but if you think about it — there must be thousands and thousands living there, and let's say three of them go back and the religion is misrepresented to them or they meet people with certain political agendas they come back and that gets reported on so strongly, and all of a sudden ordinary people get investigated and can't live their lives. And what about all the people who do the school shootings? We don't say that all white Americans are gun killers and they have an agenda against everyone else.*
>
> *Interview, 21.01.2014*

Reflecting on the information elucidated after the end of an interview , there was often a sense of a gap in the way the women spoke about the men's propensity for violence. It seemed strange that they had recounted instances where men had harmed their intimate partners or family but did not believe that these same men would harm others outside their immediate circle. There is something of a conflict between the way the women presented young men as not dangerous, and the way they view violence within their own community. This could perhaps be explained by different definitions of exactly what constitutes violence. For example, many young people described situations where violence had been used as a direct response to an issue. They gave examples of women using violence to protect their children from perceived slights, or to solve marital issues (including as a response to male instigated domestic violence). Some young people discussed the way violence is quickly resorted to by Somalis in general; they believed more than is the norm within other communities.

Additionally, there were many descriptions of how young Somali Australians feel disenfranchised, targeted unfairly by authorities, lacking in social support and mistrusted by the broader Australian community which has also been noted in other research (Fishman 2010, 7; Bailey 2015, 6). These are often-cited indicators of the potential for someone to become radicalised, however none of the young people I spoke to believed that this was a real possibility.

◊

When overt violence was raised, it was raised in the context of Somalia, not Australia. Gen 1.5 could analyse it quite deeply and offered various reasons why it might take place. On the other hand, during the field work period, a number of issues arose which were reflective of the covert violence Somalis in Melbourne are exposed to. The situation with remittances is illustrative of the ways in which covert violence functions, and the different levels on which it affects individuals. Another example of covert violence is the misleading over-representation of Somalis (and other minority groups) in crime statistics. As the agreement between a Somali community organisation and the Sherriff's office shows, possibilities to address this covert violence within the Somali community exist, however this is not the norm, and it is not always possible to address the issues that face Somalis 'in-house'.

The young people offered many reflections on the sorts of violence that face them on a daily basis. These included problematic relationships with law enforcement, difficulty gaining adequate representation if they were in trouble with the law and the problem of absent or disengaged father figures. There was a notable difference in the way that young men and young women conceived of violence, with the men stressing issues with the police, and women focusing on intimate partner violence

In terms of radicalisation, the respondents reported that they had been badly affected by media coverage of terror raids and what they believed to be suggestions that there is a problem with the Somali community in Melbourne. The girls who taught at the *dugsis* were especially surprised and disappointed by reportage suggesting that what was being taught in *dugsis* in the Australian context was dangerous, although no evidence was available to support their memories about the media reportage. They pointed out that no reporters aside from ABC and SBS representatives had ever come to meet with them and enquire about the schools.

The young people are impacted by many different forms of relational power: legal, administrative, economic, military. Being refugees places them on the receiving end of many expressions of power that are both explicit (gaining entry to a country, reporting as part of visa conditions) and implicit (difficulty in entering the labour market, learning new languages or making oneself understood). This is especially relevant to Muslims in Australia because a great deal of fear around terrorism is projected onto them and has resulted in documented abuse. Perhaps most relevant here is the media, which creates, proliferates, and reinforces public opinion around refugees, Somalis, Muslims and terrorism.

Gen 1.5 Somali Australians have a strong sense that their identity is something that is available for public consumption and critique. Because of their visible ethnic and religious difference and the increasing scrutiny focussed on individuals who share their characteristics, they felt unfairly judged by members of the mainstream Australian public. Overt violence is something that many of them had stories of from their time in Somalia, but not from the time after they settled in Australia. This violence was real to them, but at a remove from their everyday lives in Australia. This may be due to their parents' decision not to share detailed stories of their experiences with violence in Somalia so as not to burden their children.

Covert violence, on the other hand was something that many of the respondents had experienced during their time in Australia, even if they did not recognise it as such. The disadvantage they face in their status as refugees and the challenges they experience in terms of expressing their identity openly and without fear of repercussions attest to this. However, they stopped short at suggesting that the problems that face the Somali community could lead to radicalisation of young people. The respondents did not believe that the Somali community in Melbourne poses a real threat.

6

Unique Somali Ideals

As previously described, Somalis prize education very highly. This is not unusual in many migrant and refugee communities, where education is seen as the reward for the struggle to leave a homeland, and the ticket to a better life (Nunn et al. 2014; Taylor and Barton 1994; Foner 1979). However, there is something unique about the value placed on education in the Somali community in Melbourne. This could be because education has long been prized in Somalia, with both urban and rural parents sending their children to private Qur'anic schools to be educated in Islam and Arabic for many centuries. At the beginning of the 20th century, modern secular education was introduced by the British colonisers in the north and the Italians in the south, but this was reversed by Siyad Barre in 1969. All private schools were abolished under Barre's regime (Abdullahi 2001, 162), but then public schools, universities and other public institutions also began to close in the mid-1980s as tensions mounted throughout the country.

By the time Barre was toppled in 1991, all forms of education had ceased. Schools were demolished, their supplies looted, and teachers and students displaced, or even killed in the chaos that ensued. With no government in place, international NGOs and the scant-resourced communities organised what they could to keep children in schools. However, constant insecurity in a nation embroiled in a civil war made these efforts inconsistent (Birman, Trickett, and Bacchus 2001). Those born before 1980 had a chance to secure a relatively good education, either as part of the British or Italian system, or later under the regime of Siyad Barre, which allowed them the possibility of better-paid employment. But there is now at least one generation raised in Somalia with little or no formal education.

The young Somalis who arrived in Melbourne after the onset of civil war at home suffered severe disruption to their education. It is also important to recognise that their experience of engagement with the education system was gendered, from primary school through to post-secondary education. The young people affirmed the primary importance of education within Somali culture and also to Somalis in Australia:

> ***Muna***: *Somalis value education more highly than other Africans.*
>
> *Interview, 03.02.2014*
>
> ***Nafiso***: *My parents used to tell me that when Somalia was a peaceful country, they had universities; they had higher education; the Italian system. It was really well developed, and people valued education firstly because Islam teaches you to seek education — whether it's Islamic education or secular education, you were always encouraged to learn. And that really infiltrated the Somali culture and made them go towards education more than any other African country. It is the priority. It still is, even in Australia today.*
>
> *Interview, 25.01.2014*

Both Muna and Nafiso set Somalis apart from other Africans due to their prioritising of education. Nafiso references both Islam, and the access to a colonial education system as factors influencing this high regard. Both Muna and Nafiso also set Somalis apart from other Africans due to their love of education, another instance where Somalis distinguish themselves from other groups and see themselves as distinct.

In 2013, Hughes found that Somali parents were engaged with the Australian education system (despite having limited understanding of it) and reported that they were satisfied with their children's academic experience (Hughes 2013). Despite sometimes significant language barriers, Ramsden found that Somali parents made strong efforts to engage with the Australian school system in order to monitor and understand their children's academic progress. However, they were not aware of the existence of many educational resources, and due to their poor English language skills may not have benefitted from accessing them if they had known of their existence. Significantly, Ramsden found in 2008 that despite their wishes and efforts to engage with the school system, the fragmentation of the Somali community in Melbourne was a factor which limited the parents' interaction with the Australian community in general and with their children's schools (Ramsden 2008).

◊

The young women, too, believed that education is the ticket to a better life. They rated it as very important to their futures, both as a means to earn a better wage and as a way of having control in their lives, which was important to them after their fractured pasts. This finding has been echoed elsewhere, with Ramsden and Taket describing Somali parents' belief in education as a means to seize life's opportunities and to regain a sense of control over their family's future (2013). As Aaliya puts it:

> ***Aaliya***: *'It is absolutely number one for my parents'.*
>
> *Interview 21.06.2013*

In terms of their schooling experience, none of the respondents reported that there was any barrier to practicing Islam in their schools. In fact, many of them said that there were facilities where they were able to pray. Geni said that while there was no dedicated space for her to pray, she had requested that a music room be made available to her and that this happened immediately.

> ***Geni**: I remember I felt uncomfortable praying in public at school, so I asked my teacher in year 8 or maybe 9 if I could have a room. She went to the principal and he gave me a music room (we had a whole floor of little practice rooms for music) and he did it straight away, which I was really thankful about. I still remember today being so happy and feeling that they were looking out for me.*
>
> *Interview, 02.06.2014*

Education is a very important key to accessing and building social capital. This is well understood by Somalis living in Melbourne, and there was a strong sense that the benefits of education are more than simply monetary (i.e. a well-paying job as a prize). The young women interviewed were very interested in studying something that would benefit their community, such as nursing, teaching or social work.

Perhaps unusually, every female interviewed was either studying or in specialised employment that resulted from study (most often in the health sector). Most of the women had completed a bachelor degree or higher, around one-fifth had a diploma level qualification and the remainder were still studying. Of the men, two were unemployed and looking for work, about a third were employed in the construction/industrial sector, some were employed in white-collar jobs and a third were doing an apprenticeship (most commonly plumbing or electrical). In the wider Australian population, more women than men complete tertiary education and my respondents believed that the same was the case for Somalis in Melbourne. However, the available data do not support this (strongly held) belief. This will be discussed further in the following pages.

At the time of conducting interviews, I analysed the numbers of Somalis completing tertiary education or qualifications in Victoria using census data. I compared differences within the Somali community between the two census years (2006 and 2011) and then situated this in the context of the total Victorian population. I found that there has been a significant increase in the numbers of Somalis who attained a graduate qualification, bachelor degree, diploma or certificate between 2006 and 2011. For example, 117 Somali born people obtained a bachelor degree between 2006 and 2011. This represents an increase of 70.5%, a significant gain, particularly in a very small community. It must be stated that the Somali community in Melbourne is a very young one, so large numbers of people are in their teens and twenties; at the age when one would normally pursue higher education. However, in comparing this figure to the broader Victorian population (where we see an increase of 27.6% in numbers of individuals obtaining a bachelor degree), it is clear that the Somali community in Melbourne is increasingly involved with the tertiary education system. Similarly, an increase of 77.8% of Somali-born individuals gaining a graduate diploma or graduate certificate shows a deep engagement with tertiary education. The only higher qualification where the rest of the Victorian population out-paced the increase in attainment in the Somali-born population was Postgraduate degree.

Anecdotally, there is a belief within the Somali community that young women achieve much higher than men in terms of education. One young woman even claimed that Somali women go to university and Somali men go to jail. However, a deeper look at census data does not support this claim at all. Although males outperformed females in 2006 and 2011 in post-secondary educational attainment, with the notable exception that in 2011, more females had attained advanced diplomas, diplomas and certificates than males (there was a striking increase in the number of females with these qualifications between 2006 and 2011).

The contrast between the data and what was reported by both young people and older people is still surprising. I considered that my sample might be skewed, both because of its small size and because of the original links I had to the Somali community being connected with my own study and teaching. It could simply be that I interacted with a small subset of the community which did not comprise many males with university qualifications. The perceptions I witnessed may not have been representative of the entire Somali community in Melbourne.

However, it is difficult to overstate the strength of the belief that women's educational attainment was much higher than young men's educational attainment. This was a message from multiple generations in the community. Nonetheless, the message from many community members regarding the gendered differentiation of achievement in education simply did not match the census data. After consideration, there are a number of possible explanations for the disparity between the perceptions of the community and the available statistics.

One possibility is that the census data is not entirely accurate. As discussed in the first findings chapter, there other incidents of Somalis being motivated to respond to census questions untruthfully. However, in that instance, there was a clear motivation — they feared adverse consequences would result from them honestly reporting their ethnicity and religion. Here, however, it is difficult to see clear motivations for answering the census questions inaccurately.

In a small community (such as the Somali community in Melbourne) numbers can change significantly over a short period of time. This is particularly true of a young community, where proportionally high numbers of people will begin to attend educational institutions. However, the 2016 census data confirmed an increasing engagement with education from the Somali community. In 2016, of the Somali-born people aged over 15 years, 19.5% were attending educational institutions even though they had no qualifications. The rate for the total Australian population was just 8.5% (Commonwealth of Australia 2018).

The responses from both my respondents and the broader community form part of a negotiated and strategic response to their circumstances, and in some ways it is not useful to question the truth of their claims, as they form part of their reality. Perhaps this is an example of the pride of the women, their strong sense of identity, and their belief in their own ability to manage life and navigate whatever circumstances they are faced with.

For the women, it may be that the gender specific attitudes they have encountered from within their own community encourage them to believe that they are more studious than young men. The young women in particular have identified education as a tangible form of social capital which they are striving to attain. This may lead to overinflated estimates of the actual levels of educational attainment within the community.

While never in the mixed gender focus groups, in the female only groups, and in some of the extended interviews, some women were scathing of their male counterparts' academic achievements. Remarks such as 'he's only studying a trade' were common.

> ***Amal:*** *The Somali guys are lazy and there's not as much expectation for them. Education-wise there's a lot of expectation, but the expectation doesn't start from when they're young. It starts early for the girls so they can build on it. They boys have no responsibility at a young age like the girls do.*
>
> ***Hani:*** *They're spoon-fed at a young age and that carries on into adulthood. And that comes from the mother, not the father. I don't*

> *think the women are not favoured, but they are treated in another way.*
>
> **Elizabeth**: *Do you think that affects their ability to succeed in their education later on in life?*
>
> **Bilan:** *Oh, definitely. You have to be disciplined to study and you have to know how to keep going, even when it gets difficult. I think the boys, they expect other people to help them and they give up too quickly if they feel like they can't do something.*
>
> *Focus group, 02.11.2012*

This was a variation of the explanation from many of the women interviewed. They stated that they had been forced to be independent from a very early age and to assume responsibility around the house and in the care of their younger brothers, sisters and cousins (the average family size for the group interviewed was six children, which is significantly higher than Melbourne's average of 1.8). In the context of this study this was interpreted as evidence of the strong difference between the reality of Somali girls from a young age and the prevalent stereotype of the oppressed Muslim woman. The young boys, on the other hand, had far fewer responsibilities. According to many of the female respondents, the boys in Somali families are routinely spoiled, often at the expense of the girls.

> **Bilan:** *I remember one time I was trying to do my homework and it was hard, you know? And my mum, she came in and said I had to stop my homework so I could help my brother because he couldn't understand what he had to do. And I told her, 'But Iman is one year older than me! He should be able to do it on his own!' But I still had to stop my own work so I could help him with his.*
>
> *Interview, 19.05.2013*

Bilan's explanation supports Hani's earlier comment that this preferential treatment originates with the mothers, not the fathers.

While there is limited data in Australia, there have been numerous studies in the UK showing that Somali students significantly underperform compared to the mainstream population and also to other migrant groups (Kahin 1997; British Council 2007; E. Ali and Jones 2000). The situation is similar in Canada (Borzykowski 2009). However, in the United States, studies have found that Somali students are performing well, on the whole (Darboe 2003; Fennelly and Palasz 2003). As previously discussed, the sample interviewed is somewhat skewed in terms of educational attainment and aspiration. In terms of the list of desirable destinations for Somalis, the respondents said that European countries were highest on the list. Presumably then, the better-educated and connected Somalis were able to settle in the UK. It is not clear then, why their educational performance there is poor, relative to their peers.

According to the respondents, level of education was a key determinant of who got out of Somalia quickly after the outbreak of war.

> ***Elizabeth**: What enabled your families to leave Somalia before the war?*
>
> ***Hani**: I don't know why we moved. My dad was overseas in Italy studying, so maybe he could afford for us to go?*
>
> ***Sumaya**: It was always easier if you had someone overseas already.*
>
> ***Amal**: Generally, it's the people that got out in the early 90s were those who were well-off and could afford to escape. My dad left 1990. He realised that bad things were going to come. He went to Kenya. He was a real estate agent and got us out like that. I think he had some links to Kenya through his work. But someone without money, even if they could see things getting worse, there was no way out.*
>
> ***Sumaya**: My parents left early at the start of the war and they could do that because they had wealth. So in Kenya we settled*

relatively easily.

Suleiman: *I think the people who were educated could see that the situation was getting worse, and they had access to better information about when to leave and how to get out.*

Amal: *In Somalia at that time, education equalled wealth. And the people who got out early had the wealth to go. The ones that got out 96-98 went to the refugee camps in Kenya, Ethiopia, Jordan. They spread out. The wealthier you were, you had a better country to go to. To go to a European country, you were more wealthy than to go to an African country.*

Focus group, 02.11.2012

The excerpts above reveal a number of things. Firstly, and most obviously, education was a key factor in determining the ability of people to leave Somalia quickly. This was due not only to the wealth they had as a result of their education, but also, crucially, to their professional networks. Secondly, the participants' belief that the educated Somalis were better able to predict the deterioration of the situation and to act quickly to avoid becoming implicated. (This may also contribute to the extremely high value Somalis place on education, if they believe it is a tool to escape possible conflict) Finally, that there was a hierarchy of preferred destinations, which generally speaking, correlated negatively to physical proximity to Somalia. When asked about Australia's position within this hierarchy, the general response was that while it was a more preferable destination than other African countries, it was not as sought-after as a European country such as The Netherlands, or Sweden. Many of the respondents arrived on humanitarian visas, which means there were no strict educational or professional requirements from receiving countries.

Sumaya, Suleiman and Amal describe the way those with more social capital (the better-connected) in Somalia were able to predict the worsening of the situation and to act to remove themselves from it. Suleiman's comment that those better educated (and wealthier people, in Amal's estimation) had access to better information and support networks is evidence of social capital being produced by social actors for their own benefit and distributed in unequal measure. This is in agreement with Bourdieu's conception of social capital and is an example of how higher levels of social capital can be the difference between life and death in extreme situations.

The young women discussed their male counterparts' professional choices at length and showed many of the same prejudices that the boys described from the older generations.

> ***Naado**: I don't think for the boys that education is their strong point. There is a lot of Somali boys who don't think about education at all. They only want to work and play. My brother who's 31 this year never thought education was important. He was into soccer. My parents would always tell him to study and put the effort in at young age and you'd reap the rewards later. He'd get a good job and earn better money and he wouldn't have to do a trade. But he never listened so when he finished school he didn't go to university; he just did labour work and trade work. Then after that he went to Somalia, got married and then realised how important education was all of a sudden. So he did a diploma at NMIT and then to University and did accounting and finally finished last year. He tells me now; I should have listened to my mother and father. And I have 3 younger brothers and one of them has finished university. Another is going through a TAFE course and the other didn't even choose to do TAFE. He's just doing an apprenticeship. So those two will realise one day what the importance of education is and furthering your skills.*
>
> *Interview, 06.06.2014*

Naado clearly believes that trade work and TAFE are inferior to a university education. She describes university as the best choice and is dismissive of her brother who 'didn't even choose to do TAFE'.

Amal: *What's interesting is that a lot of our parents, being migrants, didn't have any access to school or uni. But the whole community places such a big importance on education for us. Not just TAFE. We have to go to university! In Somali households, university is the ultimate goal! I don't know what happened to the boys... Somehow they got left behind.*

Interview, 21.01.2014

Sumaya*: My brothers, they all went to uni – except my younger brother. I don't know what happened to him... there's always one!*

Interview, 05.05.2013

According to the women, males and females have access to the same opportunities but young girls work harder and reap the rewards. This is possibly due to the parental pressure on girls to be studious from a very young age.

Muna*: I think girls are just more interested in education.*

Amal: *And dedicated and focused. They can see things through.*

Focus group, 15.01.2014

This finding is an echo of Omar's 2011 thesis, in which he posits that a barrier to young Somali men succeeding in education is that they are not equipped to apply themselves consistently because they are not required to contribute as much as women in the home and family spheres. Therefore, the young men have not acquired the necessary skills to succeed in their studies (Y.S. Omar 2011). This is despite their parents' high expectations, including attainment of tertiary qualifications.

◊

Perhaps unsurprisingly, the males in the study did not view the situation in the same way. The group of men in the study were more likely to be doing a trade than studying at university, and they also believed that this was reflective of the Somali community in Melbourne as a whole, in contrast to the census data shown above. While they were described as lazy by their female counterparts, it is important to remember that they face a distinct set of pressures and challenges, as described above. They were much more focussed on the expectations they felt were put on them from a very young age to act properly.

> ***Absame***: *when I'm at home my mum will tell me like most of the time she tells me to act religious or whatever like she will remind me of all the stuff I have to do. And I'll do it in that moment to make them happy. But...now I'm here I want to be happy too. I'm here to learn and to make something out of myself. I was 11 when I came here. So not that young. So I still remember back home and how it used to be and stuff. So mum, she's always reminding me why I'm here and she's always on my back, like I got to study and you know you got to be good and all that. And with the trade, at least I'm doing something with myself. I'm not sitting at home, not doing bad stuff in the streets. I'm busy doing something so that's the main thing.*
>
> **Suleiman:** *My mum always goes on and on about what a young man has to do... He has to have a good job and a house and to have children. I swear, this guy is like Superman!*
>
> *Focus group, 10.02.2014*

The comments above point to the burden of expectations the young men feel from their mothers, in terms of both their responsibility to do well in Australia to make their flight from Somalia worthwhile, and also in terms of the goals their parents have for them and the (perhaps unrealistic) timeframe in which they are expected to achieve these goals.

For the young men interviewed, education was a contested and conflicted space in terms of their desires and the need to manage their parents' desires. There was a palpable sense of sadness and resignation that their parents did not appreciate that a trade is a legitimate and respectable job in Australia. The sadness, coupled with pressure from parents and grandparents, affects relationships within the home and can cause growing resentment. This was expressed in a variety of ways.

> ***Absame**: Yeah, that's it; they just don't respect the trade as much as getting a degree. It's just the mentality they grew up with. Back then it was just like anyone would do the job. They would do it the hard way and not go to school. It was just like an apprenticeship, but the wages were rubbish and the safety side of it — it was very dangerous — which makes it rubbish. And when it comes to Australia it's much more structured. They [teach you] what to do, what's right and wrong and you actually learn more.*
>
> ***Ali**: For me, it's the same as Absame, but in my case it's just like education-wise, from that point of view, parents from overseas have a lot of expectations of intellectual work like going to uni and doing stuff like doctor, or lawyer or whatnot. And they see the trade as not being number one on the list. And if you do come to Australia, it revolves around apprenticeships... and it's not something (just) anyone can do. And they can't understand that.*
>
> *Focus group, 10.02.2014*

Suleiman was even more explicit and explained that in Somalia, only lower-class people would perform physical work.

> ***Suleiman** Back home, only the poor people did the physical work. It was really dangerous, because they didn't have all the regulations like in Australia, and it was seen as a really poor and nasty thing to do.*
>
> *Focus group, 10.02.2014*

In Somalia, certain jobs were looked upon with disdain, and were only to be performed by people of a lower class. Ali's idea that the workplace in Australia 'revolves around apprenticeships' is not a false assessment. However, the 2011 census data show that 79% of apprentices were male (Australian Bureau of Statistics 2011), so it is a career path that is more common for men than women in mainstream Australian society as well. The young women are less likely to have been exposed to apprenticeships and the way they function. This fact may have informed the women's assessment that to be studying a trade is an inferior choice to attending university.

The reported differences between young men and their families regarding education choices were a source of conflict. As Absame described it:

> ***Absame***: *They're never going to respect the trade as much as uni, so I try to keep both parties happy [me and my parents] and move on.*
>
> *Focus group, 10.02.2014*

The conflict experienced by the males in relation to their education and professional choices was often coupled with a discussion about how they manage to meet their own personal needs and the needs of their parents. This led them to discussion around the need to have different parts of their personalities available to different people and the way they negotiate this contested identity.

◊

Initially the place of women among Somalis in Melbourne had not been identified as a research priority, but it was a topic that emerged early on in the fieldwork and was an important discussion point for both men and women in various ways. One effect of the disruption caused by the civil war and the great changes encountered in subsequent emigration towards the west has been to dislodge customary gender roles — very much to women's advantage, and this was discussed by the participants in great detail.

Many of the participants stated that in Somalia the gender roles were strictly outlined, but since the disruption of the civil war, this has changed significantly. In Somalia, men are considered the head of the household. They are *raganimo* — a Somali word meaning brave and also an eloquent speaker, which is especially important in Somalia due to the high value placed on oratory skills, such as reciting poetry (Abdullahi 2001, 120). Women are considered to be the managers of the household and children (Hansen 2008, 112). In Somalia, children are raised to observe these roles and also to respect their parents at all times, as both a source of *duo* (advice and blessings) and *habaar* (curse) (Kleist 2010, 189).

◊

The position of women in Somali culture was raised independently in many interviews and focus groups. In one all-female group, it took over the other topics and was discussed for over an hour. The women enjoyed pointing out examples where women have power in the household and also the public domain. One thing that stood out very clearly was the sense that the mainstream public misunderstands Somali women altogether. This is supported by Garner and El Bushra who claim that 'Somali women, whether nomadic or urban, have never been submissive, either to natural calamities or to social oppression' (Garner and El Bushra 2005, 9).

> ***Layla****: Women's position in the Somali household is stronger than other women in Islamic households, definitely.*
>
> ***Hani****: This is definitely true. My father was more educated than my mother, but he wasn't around as much. My mother was there from day one- following up and questioning us 'what are you doing with your life' and we're all a bit scared of her. She is the leader of the house. My dad is more of a guest. His character is very soft and he doesn't really know how to raise kids... no discipline. And my mum does all of that.*
>
> *Focus group, 15.01.2014*

Here, the women equate strength with position in the household. This involves child rearing, which is to be expected, but also has a strong emphasis on discipline.

However, the previous position of women in Somalia is also contested. For example, Hassan Keynan, a Somali sociologist living in Norway, explains that while 'Somali "culture" has allowed and equipped Somali men to dominate women' (citing a traditional proverb that 'a breast which contains milk cannot contain wisdom') (Haakonsen and Keynan 1995, 27), these previously well-defined gender roles have been upended. Keynan has plotted the way that some Somali women have benefitted from their migration experience, in sometimes unexpected ways. Indeed, this was supported by my own research with many Gen 1.5 women explaining that they are equally (if not more) capable and accomplished than their male peers. Similarly, the older women spoke with great joy about how they are more independent in Australia, and do not have to answer to a husband the same way they did in Somalia. There are many female-headed Somali households in Melbourne, which of course removes the requirement of answering to a husband - some husbands are not present, having been lost in the war or never reunited with their family in Australia. However even those women who are married were very clear that they have significantly more power in Australia than they would have had in Somalia.

However, the young women claimed that in comparison to other Muslims, Somalis have always afforded women greater authority. Many cited the fact that Somali women can seek a divorce as evidence for this, along with the high proportion of women in Somalia who work outside the household.

Some of the women speculated that the position of women was very different in other Muslim households:

> ***Hani****: I used to talk to my Arab friends about our parents and they would always say that their fathers disciplined them and they would be scared of them and they didn't have such a close relationship with their fathers because they were afraid. And I used to tell them it was the opposite in our house. Even if I stayed out all night — I would have to answer to my mother.*
>
> ***Sumaya****: They have self-belief. I don't know where it comes from but it's very strong. My dad is very respected in his tribe but my mum is equally respected in her sphere as well. There is no expectation that the man does everything, and the woman sits at home. She has her own business. She's not put down!*
>
> *Focus group, 15.01.2014*

Here, Sumaya affords equal weight to the work that is done inside the house and outside. There was a sense of respect when describing the work involved in running a household and rearing children. However, this work did not prevent women from also pursuing paid work outside the household and running business enterprises.

> ***Amal:*** *Somali women have a very strong character — whether it's discipline, education, community life; they're very involved.*
>
> ***Sumaya****: My mum controls the finances of the house — she used to help me with homework and at school. Most things she did in the home.*
>
> *Focus group, 15.01.2014*

A strong matriarch seems to be at the heart of many Somali households in Melbourne. While the assumption was this would be because of the high numbers of single mothers, most of the young people identified their mothers as the head of the house, regardless of the presence of a father. I asked them if women had been made strong by the prolonged conflict in Somalia.

> ***Hani****: I don't know if it's post-war. I think it's a woman's characteristic. It's a culture thing. In Somali culture, women are able to*

divorce and remarry and that's not the case in many Muslim cultures. That shows how much power women have.

Interview, 22.09.2014

***Sumaya**: They're definitely not limited. Islam was never really implemented properly into Somalia, was it? Properly. It was more culture.*

Interview, 29.11.2014

While Hani describes women's power and pride as a Somali characteristic, Sumaya believes that it is in the nature of Islam to oppress women, or deny them some aspects of power and that it is a failure to implement Islam fully that has allowed Somali women to possess the power they do. In previous chapters, I have described how the arrival of Islam in Somalia in the 7th century did not have as large an impact as has been claimed. Certainly, the fact that large-scale conversions to Islam did not take place until some 500 years later could be construed as evidence that Somali culture had time to flourish alongside but distinct from Islam before Somalis converted fully to the religion. The suggestion that Somalis still engage with tribal customs and rituals which existed prior to Islam's implementation is an intriguing one, and an avenue which is ripe for further research. Sumaya's belief that Islam is inherently sexist, and Somali women have benefitted from the incomplete implementation of Islam was not held by all the young people in the study, with many highlighting their belief that sexism can arise in Islam when it is not practiced properly.

Hani believes that Somali women are fundamentally different from Somali men.

***Hani**: I think Somali women have more pride in them. It's a national characteristic! I don't think any Somali woman would sit at home and cry about being abused by her husband. She wouldn't accept it. She would take a stand. She would either bash him up or* *call the police and the authorities on him. She is not belittled. She has a pride about her that she will not be discriminated against and abused.*

Interview, 22.09.2014

Aaliya similarly described how her mother refused to be oppressed by her father when she wanted to end her marriage.

> ***Aaliya**: My mother married when she was 18 or 19 and then she had 5 children close together and then she left. And she was unlike my father she was an influential woman, you know some of her brothers were in the government. She was city, she was working, she was a graduate from high school, and she was working for the army. So my father was different culturally so there is a clash between cultures. My father, where he came from a woman doesn't have that independence.*
>
> ***Elizabeth:** So your mother was urban?*
>
> ***Aaliya**: Yeah, she was urban, and my father I couldn't say he was like from the bush but you know he left from the village in Ethiopia when he was 16 but somehow his mentality doesn't change that much from the way he sees women. He was of the belief that women should not work and should stay at home. And my mum was urban, and she was a very proud woman. So she asked him he will either give her enough money to build her a house or he will allow her to work. She can't support herself and her children and he doesn't allow either one of the two so she has to get out from the marriage.*
>
> *Interview, 21.06.2013*

Layla agrees that women are treated differently in other Muslim cultures:

> ***Layla**: When I went to uni I had that feeling when I made friends with other Muslim girls. The women were very different. And I think some cultures used Islam to advantage the men and put them higher than the women. You'd hear certain things and they say*

> *'Oh... Islamically... I'm not permitted to do that' And you think, 'that's not Islam!' They teach you that to keep you down. But I could still be friends with them and we discussed it really openly.*
>
> *Interview, 03.02.2014*

Here, Layla suggests that it is the implementation of Islam which does this, saying 'They teach you that to keep you down'. While Layla describes the timid nature of her non-Somali Muslim friends, she also claims she is able to discuss their differences 'really openly'. However, she then continued on to say,

> ***Layla**: After I left uni though, they weren't really my friends any more. I would sometimes feel so frustrated with them, that they wouldn't express themselves and work to get what they wanted.*
>
> *Interview, 03.02.2014*

The above comments show clearly the breadth of cultural and religious practice across the broader Muslim world. These practices change both across time and space. When asked about the situation for women in Somalia now, the answer was different.

> ***Nafiso:** In Somalia at the moment it's so unstable and there are so many radical groups coming and demanding things, and then they get overturned and more radicals come and demand more things. So I don't know how it is for women there.*
>
> *Interview, 25.01.2014*

This response indicates that the power women are accorded in Australia may no longer exist in Somalia as a result of the implementation of radical Islam. So there are two very different interpretations of Islam in play. The first, which Sumaya identifies as an incorrect or incomplete application of Islam, allows women power and agency. Layla agrees that Islam is being manipulated to the detriment of women. The second, which is being implemented in Somalia now by the 'radicals', does not allow women free agency. Ironically, it seems that this is the way the young Somali women believe Islam functions in many other Muslim countries, even if it is not their preferred implementation of Islam.

The women highlighted again the importance of the differences in the way that boys and girls are raised, but this time offered this difference as a practical reason for female power in Somali culture:

> ***Hani:*** *They're spoon-fed at a young age and that carries on into adulthood... I don't think the women are not favoured, but they are treated in another way. And this means they know how to work hard and to make a success of themselves. And they know how to get what they want later on in life.*
>
> *Focus group, 15.01.2014*

It was often raised that the young women felt they had 'something to prove' both to their parents, the Somali community and the mainstream Australian community as well. As Layla puts it:

> ***Layla****: The way I see it is this. I have so many crosses against me. Number one is my religion. Number two is because I'm a girl. Number three is because I arrived here when I was already 9 years old. And I have to prove myself to so many different people. I have to say to my parents, 'Yes I can be as much of a success as my brothers'. Then I have to show the other people at school and at uni that I can achieve and then after that I need to set an example. So I will work hard to be a success.*
>
> *Interview, 03.02.2014*

This is an example of a positive response to the challenges faced by those who occupy contested identities. In this case, Layla uses the expectations that others have of her as motivation to succeed in order to prove herself. For Layla, gender is another identity that must be negotiated (in addition to 'refugee' and 'Muslim'), and she chooses to use it as extra incentive to achieve. While Layla describes the many different expectations people have of her and the way she has strived to meet and exceed them, Amal thinks otherwise about the measure of success:

> ***Amal:*** *I disagree. What I set to be a success might be different to other people. For Somalis, if you finish university, that's success and if you don't you have failed. But many boys are not going to uni. They do trades and doing other things. But at home the trades were done by lower class people. So I feel like they're doing a lot! They're learning a profession, but they come home, and they're not respected. They are treated as less.*
>
> ***Sumaya****: They do a lot of things. They set up the soccer here and that's like a massive success. There are so many options for boys here.*
>
> ***Hani****: Some of them are definitely trying to improve themselves, and if they don't succeed in the academic section, they do something else.*
>
> *Focus group, 15.01.2014*

The young women highlighted the role that gender plays in the construction of identities for males as well. As Amal explained, the expectation that all young men will graduate from university can have damaging consequences for those who wish to pursue other careers. The perception that they have failed was one that the young men described as well. Sumaya points to the formation of the Australian Somali Football Association (ASFA), which has a number of teams around Melbourne. It is widely celebrated as an inclusive sporting organisation and was mentioned many times during my fieldwork as something for the Somali community in Melbourne to be proud of.

◊

The great changes brought about by the migration experience have also had a significant effect on Somali men. The situation in Norway has been described thus:

> Many believe that the changes taking place in gender relations are too radical and too destabilizing. They view the growing empowerment of women as a serious threat to their authority and dignity and, by extension, as a threat to the moral and cultural norms and traditions of Somali society. They complain about humiliation and lack of respect, marginalization and expulsion, orders being given by their wives, loss of family coherence and values and confusion and disorientation in the way children are brought up. (Haakonsen and Keynan 1995).

A decade later, Ladan Affi made very similar findings regarding Somalis who had moved to Canada (Affi 2005). And in Australia, gender relations as interpreted by men from the Horn of Africa (Sudan, Somalia, Eritrea, and Ethiopia) have also been examined. These migrants and refugee men are suffering a sense of marginalisation and even ostracism, summed up in the following extract from a conversation: '[In Australia] what comes first are the women, then children, cats, dogs, followed by men' (Muchoki 2013). It is important to note that this shift within the Somali community in Melbourne is also taking place against a backdrop of increasing challenges to traditional masculinity in mainstream society. Challenges to what has been understood to be "male" and "masculine" are arising with greater frequency, to the point where it is common to speak of a 'crisis of masculinity', and 'toxic masculinity'.

In many discussions, it was notable how much the young men deferred to the women in their lives, sisters, mothers, and grandmothers.

> ***Bashir**: Well, I'm engaged now, but this was organised by my mum. She made the visits to the family and I think she chose the girl a long time ago too. Of course, she asked me what I thought,*

> *but I just think of it this way: Who knows you better than your own mother?*
>
> *Focus group, 02.11.2012*

This statement displays Bashir's willingness to go along with plans that were organised by his mother, even though it is a situation that concerns him intimately and profoundly. His acceptance of an arranged marriage is very telling in terms of his position as a member of Gen 1.5. He is a successful graphic designer with a bachelor degree, working in a white-collar environment, surrounded by what he calls 'Anglos'. Despite his adaptation and settlement into what he acknowledges is a very 'white' environment, he accepts his mother's decision about who would make an acceptable wife for him. Bashir's case was significant for me as an example of the tension of the position occupied by Gen 1.5. He is in some ways very Australian in his outlook and his daily life, but in this context at least, he is very Somali.

Iman reported that his mother as equally influential:

> ***Iman**: The one who controls our house is definitely my mum. She is the one who tells us about what we should study, and how we should look after our money. My dad works full-time but she is only part-time, and it seems like she knows everything that goes on in our house.*
>
> *Interview, 27.04.2014*

Some of the men explained that they didn't always like the way women had control in their lives:

> ***Suleiman:** My other Arab friends, they have a really different relationship with their mothers. They are much more independent and they check with their father before they do something. Like I still have to tell my mum every weekend if I want to play soccer. She doesn't understand that I'm 22 now; I'm not a kid anymore.*

Interview, 24.04.2014

Interestingly, Suleiman would be more willing to run his plans by his father, but he feels resentful that he has to discuss them with his mother. Because all my unmarried respondents lived at home with their parents, they very much obeyed the rules set by the women in their family.

One of the young men who did not wish to be recorded told me that he doesn't have a father in Australia. It is not known what happened to him, but the family believes that he was killed in conflict in Somalia. He described how growing up without a father proved to be an immense challenge to his identity as he did not have anyone to look up to or imitate. A recent study in London contrasts the situation of young Somali men and women in this context:

> Another important outcome following the loss of a father is a lack of role models for many Somali boys. While many Somali women are enjoying a new sense of freedom and Somali girls are exploiting new opportunities in education, boys can experience a sense of alienation from the system and struggle for a sense of identity. (Harding, Clarke, and Chappell 2007, 7).

Previously, the level of pressure from grandparents and parents, and the expectation they have of their children and grandchildren has been discussed. However, the above examples also demonstrate the conflicting expectations that exist between peers in the Somali community. It seems that the women and the men have different expectations and conceptions of what a positive professional trajectory looks like. There appears also to be some confusion and resentment around who occupies what roles around the home. These aspects of Somali life, which take some navigation for the actors, add more compounding factors to the contested space that informs their expressions of identity. Indeed, this adds a further challenging dimension (from within the community) to their already multifaceted contested identities. It seems that being studious is culturally more acceptable for girls. It matches the expectations of their parents, that they are more mature and better able to manage the requirements of the outside world.

◊

The young people occupy contested identities, and used different strategies to enable them to move between the different spheres of their lives, most notably in their interactions with their parents and with the mainstream Australian community. However, they did so with varying degrees of success and their experiences were gendered. Many felt the burden of competing expectations and struggled to integrate their many identities. While some accepted that this was reality for many people, not just migrants and people who look different from mainstream Australians, others felt it was unjust that they had to tailor their personality to different situations.

Education is highly valued by Somalis in Melbourne to the point where it becomes a distinguishing factor in their identity, and something they believe sets them apart from other African communities. According to respondents, level of education (and as a result of education, increased wealth and better networks) was a key determinant in who was able to leave Somalia quickly when the political situation began to deteriorate in the late 1980s and early 1990s.

The young women were sometimes dismissive of their male counterparts' success in education. They claimed that there are lower expectations of Somali boys to help around the house and be involved in family life, and that they are therefore less equipped to persevere with education. While the young men did not explicitly agree with the women's accounts, they described the burden of the high expectations their parents place upon them from a young age. The men in a trade profession were very aware (in their own minds) that they had fallen short of their parents' expectations. They explained their inability to assure their parents that working in a trade is a viable and respectable occupation in Australia, and that they felt their parents would always be disappointed they had not attended university.

The place of women has evolved dramatically between Somalia and Australia. While some argue that Somali society had strictly defined roles for men and women, these have been eroded by political, cultural, and social flux in Somalia itself, and by the journey from Somalia to other countries where women occupy many different roles. Both men and women described the inner strength of Somali women and the fact that in Australia, many women are 'head of the household'. They contrasted with to other Muslim families, where they believe children report to their fathers and are disciplined by them. Some women described how their mothers and other women had successfully sought divorce as evidence of women's strength and ability to be masters of their own destiny.

The young men described the success of their sisters, wives, and cousins in Australia. This was in terms of education, professional lives, and ability to set goals and achieve them. However, this was not always viewed in a positive light, with some young men expressing frustration at the way their lives were directed by women. In addition, the young men have encountered significant difficulties and feelings of alienation because of the perceived success of the women. There was a notable lack of understanding and communication between men and women regarding these issues.

III – Concluding reflections

7

Identity and suspicion

Gen 1.5 Somali Australians must negotiate a complex path in the expression of their identities. There are manifold and often competing facets to the way in which their expressions of identity are configured. Here, it is worth remembering the description of power and ideology as offered by Foucault; that power is intricately connected with human activity. In Foucault's words 'Power is everywhere; not because it embraces everything, but because it comes from everywhere' (Foucault 1998 [1976], 93). Connecting this with the formation of self-identity, Somali Gen 1.5 certainly present a multifaceted case. Power, in the form of implicit ideology, comes from everywhere. But, for them, 'everywhere' represents so many directions that have the potential to form their conception of self — migrant, refugee, Muslim, African, Australian, multicultural, and so on. For these young people, their conception of themselves is intricately tied up with their perception of the world and orientation within the world and how they are able to orient themselves with respect to the discursive categories made possible for them.

It is important to point out here that it took some time to establish a relationship which enabled speaking more frankly with the young people about the issues that confronted them in terms of balancing family expectations with the expectations they felt from other quarters. In the first instance, they were keen to point out that they were proud of their roots and culture and focussed on the many positive aspects of their familial relationships. It was necessary to ask them further questions such as 'Is there anything your parents don't understand about your life in Melbourne?' for them to begin to unpack their experience a little more. This led me to question if they were trying to protect their parents? Or perhaps themselves from being portrayed as immigrant kids going off the rails?

After some follow up interviews, there was a sense that their reticence to speak about certain issues was not so much a conscious decision, rather a result of the fact that many had not explicitly thought about these issues. To them their lives are normal, and perhaps not worthy of dissection and presentation. It is possible that for some respondents at least, the conversations encouraged them to think about themselves in a way they had not done before.

> ***Filad:*** *I think everyone has difficulties finding out who they are in life, no matter where they come from. But for us, it's like we have to be one person for our parents, one person for our grandparents, one person for our friends, one person for our colleagues. It's hard to find the person you can be in all situations.*
>
> *Interview, 19.05.2014*

Here, Filad has summed up the struggles she faces in negotiating her identity on a day-to-day basis. Other respondents touched on similar themes to those mentioned above, telling me that they were torn between their families and the outside world. According to Loukia Sarroub, Muslim youth are 'triangulators of identity, and, as a result, culture is enacted in the in-between places they occupy in their home and school worlds' (Sarroub 2005, 7). Sarroub's work with immigrant Yemeni girls in the US is a great help to understanding the experiences of Somali youth and the fact that their identity construction does not only occur in response to or in conflict with white mainstream society. It also occurs within their families, across generations, and within their communities (Sarroub 2005, 7). Filad refers to this above, saying she feels the need to be one person for her parents and another person for her grandparents. She is struggling to meet the expectations of different generations within her community. Somali Gen 1.5ers must integrate many distinct identities including Muslim, visibly different refugee, young person and Gen 1.5. Their identities are contested and complex. This is the case for many young people but the forces that act on them are more numerous and much more powerful than those that affect mainstream young people.

Layla spoke about the need to fuse identities:

> ***Layla**: You just have to be able to get to a point where you know who you are to different people and join those individual personalities up to get the one person. You can take bad and good things from different situations and the different expectations we have on us all the time. I don't know, maybe it's possible to join the good things together? And then you could become some kind of super woman! Laughs... But you got to protect your own culture and who you really are. That's important.*
>
> *Focus group, 03.02.2014*

Layla's comments above are rich and detailed in terms of explaining how she sees herself in light of the competing expectations placed upon her. She acknowledges that it might be possible to maintain a consistent and coherent sense of self, but is perhaps a little sarcastic or gently mocking of the idea that she can take the 'good things' to make 'some kind of superwoman'. Although she laughed as she spoke about this issue, there was a sense that her identity is in flux, and that she is very conscious in her strategic management of this fluidity. Her final comments regarding her own culture and who she really is show how tightly she holds onto her Somali identity, and how much this forms a core part of her sense of self.

In terms of acceptance by the mainstream community, there were varied responses from the young men.

> **Omar**: *Yeah, I found that in the wider community, I wasn't accepted as an Australian, you know? I could say I was an Aussie as much as I liked, wear the green and gold as much as I liked, but no matter what, around my friends, I was never considered an Australian. I went to actually a very multicultural school, so there was a lot of Islanders, Arabs, Somalis. It was very diverse. It was called Banksia Secondary College; it's shut down now. But it was a very diverse school ... and if ever the teacher would be like 'Omar what nationality are you?' I'd answer 'I'm Australian.' She's like 'But, your background', and so I'd tell her I'm of Somali background and I consider myself as an Australian. So that was difficult, and then when I'd go home, I'm Somali but my parents would be [telling me] 'You act like an Australian, you don't even talk your own language at home. You got to talk your own language'.*
>
> *Group interview, 11.05.2014*

Omar's response indicates his willingness and desire to identify as Australian, and the difficulty he faced when questioned about this identification. He acknowledges his background but reaffirms his desire to be considered Australian. However, he contrasts this denial of his Australian identity in the public sphere with his parents' idea that he was too Australian inside the home.

Interestingly, one of the main identifiers for Omar (above) in terms of 'Australian-ness' was the ability and willingness to 'wear the green and gold'. Sport has long been acknowledged as a 'means and marker of integration' (Noble and Taber 2002). It was clear that sport was a place where the young men felt able to express their Australian identity.

> **Mansuur**: *I just love the AFL football we have here. It's a totally new game. And I know the stats and the scores. So this is something I can talk about with my Anglo friends. At first they were surprised*

> *that I knew what it is [Australian Football], but now it's something we can discuss all the time.*
>
> *Interview 17.05.2014*

When the men discussed elements of Australian culture they valued, sport was often referenced. Bashir suggested that this was because in the refugee camps, the children did not have a structured school life, or the facilities to study.

> ***Bashir**: So we would all get together, like, maybe 50 kids or more and play Soccer. We could always find a soccer ball to kick around and it was great! I mean, the camps were really hard. It wasn't all fun, but we had the best time with each other.*
>
> *Focus group, 02.11.2012*

But a love of sport is not enough to bridge all the differences between Somali Gen 1.5ers and their peers.

> ***Ali**: I would say the Europeans; the wogs were accepted more as Australians rather than the Arabs and the Somalis and I thought that was because of our different faiths. With the Arabs, the Lebanese were Muslims just like the East Africans and Somalis so during lunch time we'd all take the time out to go pray... but they had a lot more similarities with the wogs that were non-Muslim because you know, they would eat the food from the canteen, where we wouldn't eat it. We'd bring foods from home because we had to eat halal. So they were accepted more as Australians than us. But at the end of the day, whenever there was multicultural day and everyone was putting their different culture out in public, the Europeans did the same thing. So that was the only day it felt like 'They're just like us too'.*
>
> *Group interview, 28.05.2014*

Ali first says that he believes that the Europeans (who were often referred to as 'wogs' without any derision or distinction in the discussions) were more accepted because they were not of a different faith. He highlights the fact that all the Muslims would take the time to pray at lunchtime. Here, we see once again the lived practice of Islam, where the physical and practical commitment to Islam recreates the difference between them and their peers, through everyday practice. Ali presented a hierarchy of which ethnic backgrounds were most acceptable in his school. This response has echoes of the way multiculturalism has functioned in Australia in the past. There are obvious parallels here between the perceived hierarchy of migrants and the hierarchy of acceptable migrants under the White Australia Policy, which allowed migration based on European appearance. At that time, these demarcations were explicit and celebrated as a good method for Australia to expand its population. While this is no longer the case, Ali's comment reveals that he, at least, believes that there are some migrants that are more acceptable than others.

Another revealing comment came from Mohamed:

> ***Mohamed**: The thing is, everybody in Australia is always talking about being tolerant. But how tolerant can they be? I think there are some people it is too hard to tolerate.*
>
> ***Elizabeth**: What sort of people are they?*
>
> ***Mohamed**: You know, the people who do bad things, or who are too different?*
>
> ***Elizabeth**: Too different?*
>
> ***Mohamed**: Yeah, like different skin, different religion, that's not OK. Different food and music is fine though.*
>
> *Interview, 20.03.2014*

This analysis invites us to question the use of 'tolerance' as something Australian multiculturalism has promoted (Spaaij 2012, 1520). Mohamed was quite matter-of-fact in his assessment of what sorts of characteristics were tolerated in Australia, however he was also faintly sarcastic about what people it is 'too hard to tolerate'. Ghassan Hage points out the insidious inner meanings of the term 'tolerance'. Far from being a term we should be proud of, he argues that it reflects our narrow and insular ideals (Hage 1998). As Mohamed puts it, 'Different skin, different religion, that's not ok.' Our 'tolerance' does extend, however, to foreign food and music. Similar to Ali's comments above, there is a sense here that there is a hierarchy of acceptable migrants and that Somalis are low in the ranking. This idea came up quite regularly during the interviews, leading to an interesting comparison: contrasting the hierarchy of ideal places to migrate to after leaving Somalia, and the reception of Somalis in Australia, a place that was high in the ranking of ideal destinations.

Suleiman was very sure of the need to respect and maintain his culture:

> ***Suleiman*** *Personally I think it's good to hold on to your culture... you know, you have something different to offer the country you've become a national to. I might be an Australian, but just like the Italians, you go to Lygon Street, you walk along, there's different meals... a different way of life. So some part of my culture, people might like it if I hold on to it, but if I just automatically disregard my own culture, they won't have an appreciation for it. But there are things that I like and accept about the Australian culture, which I've come to. Like the AFL, it's not a sport that's recognised by the whole world but it's a really nice game.*
>
> *Focus group, 10.02.2014*

Suleiman's statement stresses the need to value your own culture if you expect others to value it too. It also recognises that not every part of a culture will be appreciated and adopted by outsiders.

Compiling this chapter, it was interesting to note that while many young men referenced sport as a way of connecting with mainstream Australians (and other minority groups), the young women did not discuss sport, or any particular activity which they felt brought them closer to their peers and colleagues. It is not culturally acceptable for Somali women to play football, although there are some women involved in the Somali football association in Melbourne in administrative positions. Upon reflection, it seems that the young women in this study had largely more positive relationships with members of the mainstream population (particularly in the school setting) and did not feel the need to establish connections through other avenues.

There was much discussion about the presentation of identity to Somali parents and extended family. Many of the young people described their parents not understanding their perspectives. Many other reports and studies have found that Somalis experience significant intergenerational conflict due to Somali youth having different life experiences and expectations to their parents (J. Smith 2008; Keating and Simons 2008; Omar 2011; Harding, Clarke, and Chappell 2007). Absame explains that he feels held back in his attempts to blend into Australian culture by his family:

> ***Absame***: *For me it's more like my mum. She expects me to be very religious and when I'm with her to act proper Somali and I can't talk English, she expects me to speak the Somali tongue. But when I'm at work I just act normal, and talk normal English.*
>
> *Focus group, 10.02.2014*

Here, Absame also identifies as Australian. That is what is 'normal' for him. It seems that being Australian is easier and more relaxed than being 'proper Somali', and that, for his mother at least, it is not possible to be 'proper Somali' while speaking English. This was something that many older people discussed , and is indeed a very common migrant and refugee experience. The parents and first-generation arrivals had a clear idea of how their children should behave, and what are acceptable choices for them to make.

The following generations (including the respondents) are exposed to many new experiences and have the opportunity to lead very different lives from the ones their parents had envisaged for them. There is something of a tension here in that many older Somalis in this study had left Somalia in order to ensure a better life for their children: one with more freedom and opportunities. However, they did not recognise the breadth of opportunity available to their children in Australia.

This was something that the mothers spoken to had serious concerns about, and these concerns for the most part, were confined to their sons rather than their daughters. As mentioned in the previous chapter, the mothers were much more confident in their daughters' abilities to navigate life successfully. Their focus and attention were directed firmly towards their sons. The pressure felt by my male participants was accordingly higher than the pressure felt by my female participants.

The difference between home life and professional life was highlighted by many of the males in this study. In general, their level of concern was directly related to their occupation: Those who worked in the trades or industrial sectors found a greater discrepancy between the expectations at work and at home than those in a white-collar profession. However, this was not universally true. Abdinoor states:

> ***Abdinoor****: Well me personally, I wasn't born here. I came here when I was five. So I know what my expectation level is at home. So like, the way I speak at home I am expected to know the whole Somali community. But the younger ones, the ones who were born here, everyone is a bit more lenient with them. But I'm just comfortable. I sort of have to, I won't say fake, but when I work, I do trade, plumbing. The way I am at home, that's me but at work I have to put on a different character to fit in. But I don't have to do that at home.*
>
> *Group interview, 11.05.2014*

Here, Abdinoor acknowledges that he behaves differently at home and in the workplace. But he is more comfortable with the expectations he has at home than those that are present in the workplace. This is in direct contrast to Absame's experience of being 'normal' in the workplace and altering his behaviour when at home with his mother.

Iman's experience was different again:

> ***Iman****: Well, I work as a youth social worker, you know? And in our area [North Melbourne], we're working with lots and lots of multicultural youth. So it's actually a topic of interest in the office and when we're out on the street. The only thing is that my parents used to think that this was women's work, not work for a man. I spent a lot of time talking to them about what I do to make them see that it is a good job to have.*
>
> *Interview, 27.04.2014*

Iman points out that he is immersed in a multicultural world at home and at work, so the transition for him is presumably easier. But he also explains that he needed to educate his parents about his chosen career in order for them to have an understanding and acceptance of his work.

The three young men above have similar experiences in that they are inhabiting different parts of their identity in response to different external stimulus. However, they feel varying levels of comfort in the different domains. While some feel more comfortable in the workplace, others are more at ease in the home.

Bashir, a graphic designer, reports as follows:

> ***Bashir****: I work in a really white office. When I was at Uni it was pretty Anglo too, so I was used to it. But it's not really a problem for me. Honestly, the issue doesn't come up except for Ramadan when they ask why I don't have [my] lunch with me.*
>
> *Focus group, 02.11.2012*

Here, despite his acknowledgement of visible difference, Bashir is not concerned about shifting between public and private identities. This situational identity allows him to interact comfortably with a wide range of people in his life. It enables him to know how to act or how not to act, and informs his expectations of situations

Mansuur described how the navigation of contested identity becomes easier with practice.

> ***Mansuur**: It was harder when I was younger. But now they don't really care as much, but they're still really aware of it. But it's like getting used to two cultures and walking the fine line is not the easiest thing. But once you get the hang of it, you just cruise through.*
>
> *Focus group, 10.11.2012*

But Mohamed was frustrated with the need to tailor his responses to different situations.

> ***Mohamed**: It just sometimes gets me so exhausted that I have to be one person at home, another person with my Somali friends, then another one at work, and another one with the Aussies I know. I wish I could be the same person all the time, but that's not going to happen.*
>
> *Group interview, 28.05.2014*

Mohamed seems to assume here that he is unusual in needing to present himself differently in different contexts. His wish to be 'the same person all the time' is at odds with current scholarly theories of identity, however it was clear to me that he believes that mainstream Australians do not need to alter the way they present themselves in different contexts. He wished to be able to present a singular version of his 'authentic self' in the same way he believes mainstream Australians can.

The question of career choices kept arising in the discussion around negotiating public and private identities.

> ***Mansuur**: I've found balancing the two ways, the old way and the new way can be a bit tricky at times and you have to live a double life in a sense, because I found that growing up while I was studying through high school, I really didn't want to keep studying, I wanted to...do a trade but I knew that would be frowned upon and people would say 'Why don't you study instead?' They wouldn't give the trades an opportunity because if you're a tradesman back in Somalia you're considered a second-class citizen. Your job is not as important as a corporate job, you know, the guy wearing a tux. There is much more of a class difference in the trades back home. And the pay rate wasn't high back home. And there wasn't small businesses and things like that. So I was pretending a bit at school, and I actually got the apprenticeship without talking to my parents at all.*
>
> *Focus group, 10.11.2012*

Much like Absame's experience above, Mansuur was not able to communicate his wishes adequately to his parents. He also stresses that trades are not highly valued by Somalis, However, unlike Iman, he was not able to explain why things are different in Australia, and why he did not wish to go to university. In the conversations with Mansuur, it became clear that he felt particularly torn between the life his parents expected him to have, and the life he wished to lead in Australia. He was a very good example of a Gen 1.5er who felt pressured by straddling two worlds. This is particularly relevant for Gen 1.5 Somali Australians, because they usually live at home until marriage. Therefore, their parents are very present in their lives at a time when they are exercising greater and greater independence. Note that Mansuur pursued his apprenticeship without telling his parents about it, which indicates he was able to make a choice that was right for him despite knowing that his parents would not be happy with that choice.

Ishaar describes how, even though he is studying at a tertiary level, some members of his family are not pleased because he is studying a modern rather than a traditional course.

> ***Ishaar***: *I still went to university, but I decided to do media instead of doctor, or engineer or something like that. So… this is something new, media to my family wasn't interesting because back home we look at people who do certain trades and occupations, they're not viewed as highly as someone who is a doctor or a teacher… and having my grandmother live with me at home, she doesn't speak any English. And she doesn't understand what we can study these days… what is available to us.*
>
> *Group interview, 11.08.2014*

In general, there was a level of resentment among the men pursuing a trade or working in the industrial sector that their skills were not appreciated by their families. They also admitted jealousy of their sisters (many of whom are teachers, nurses or working in the medical administration field) for the way their choice of career was accepted and celebrated. Interestingly, in Ishaar's case, despite his choice of study requiring a university qualification, his family equated it with undesirable trade work because it was unfamiliar to them. This supports Yusuf Omar's findings about Somali youth in Minneapolis and Melbourne. He found that the young men believed their parents' expectations to be unrealistic, and not take into account the diverse range of educational and professional opportunities available outside university (Omar 2011).

> ***Ishaar***: *I came here when I was 5 in 1998 and my mum's a single mum and I have 3 older sisters. So living in a house full of women is hard... And the expectation that my mum had, because she saw my sisters, and they were a bit older when they came here. Especially my oldest sister. She took initiative straightaway saying, 'Mum's by herself…' so she went to uni, got a degree. She did nursing and my other sister is a teacher and the other one is still studying. But I was completely different. I was different. That's not what I wanted to do. But my mum, back home she worked for the*

UNDP, so she was expecting me to be educated, be proper. Go to university, do this do that.

Group interview, 11.08.2014

Ishaar's family in Somalia was presumably well educated and connected for his mother to work for the UNDP. For Ishaar's family, his sister's choices of nursing and teaching were acceptable career paths to pursue. His younger sister is also studying at university in an unspecified course. The traditional nature of his sisters' career paths seems to equate to success for his family, however his choice of media studies does not. This is despite media studies being a course that is generally considered respectable in Australia, and certainly not at a lower level than nursing or teaching. It is possible that his family does not see it as an appropriate career choice for a man. However, it is possible that the difficulty for Ishaar's mother stems from the fact that his university course is a recent creation and would not have existed in Somalia. It is most likely unfamiliarity which makes Ishaar's mother anxious about his choice.

The expression of identity is at the heart of this book, and the above section has shown that it can be challenging for Gen 1.5 Somalis in Melbourne to inhabit their identities when confronted with the many different pressures upon them. These expectations come from within and outside their ethnic community. The young people discussed the different people they needed to be for their parents and grandparents, and among their Somali Australian peers.

These experiences were heavily affected by gender. The young women acknowledged the difficulties they faced in relation to competing expectations, however these difficulties were multiplied for the males. For example, some young men spoke about how they were uncomfortable about expressing their Muslim identity in the workplace. One way they bridged the divide between themselves and mainstream Australians was through a shared interest in sport, particularly Australian Rules football. However, they also identified a perceived hierarchy of minority groups in Australia, and believed they fell towards the lower end of the hierarchy due to their cultural, religious, and physical differences. One source of continued frustration for the young men in particular was the lack of support from their families in respect of their educational and professional choices.

◊

This study started as a personal interest project in 2010. Sadly, with each year that passed, the themes became more and more salient, politicised, and prominent on the public agenda. The pressures on the young people in this study with have increased in accordance with the level of public scrutiny on them.

Overall, the sheer scale of the effort that Somali Gen 1.5ers in Melbourne have to go to, to inhabit their contested identities, the awareness they have about these identities and the way they have been represented is astounding. This is not an abstract awareness; rather it permeates everyday interactions, for example, in explaining your citizenship to a taxi driver, or leaving the lunchroom at work when the conversation turns to religion. This study has critically examined the representation of Somalis by others and analysed how their expression of identity differs from these representations. Even though I did not set out to dispel myths about this particular population, one of the findings was that their identity expression was vastly different to common representations of them.

The identities of Gen 1.5 Somalis in Melbourne are constructed in the context of myriad ideological influences and discursive categories. The way the implicit power relations in society affect these young people is unique. Representations of Somalis by others shape Gen 1.5, as they forge and express their identities. They are often forced to consider themselves in terms of the categories that others project onto them.

The young people had a deep engagement with Islam. Many described it as the thing that defined them, and they were worried about how Islam is perceived by mainstream Australian. This included widespread suspicions that actively practicing Muslims are likely to commit acts of terrorism. Within the Somali community in Melbourne, the vast majority of women are veiled and some of the women were frustrated that the veil is the only thing people see about them, to the point that it negates other facets of their person. Although there were many challenges to their participation in Islamic life while living in a Muslim minority country, the young people were proud of this particular aspect of their identities. They lived their religion in a physical and practical way, determining what decisions to make based on Islamic values, dressing modestly and engaging in daily prayer. Their engagement with Islam was far more significant than their engagement with Somali culture. In fact, they made some disparaging remarks about the cultural artefacts which their parents found important, and it was clear that their identity was much more reliant on Islam and their religious practices than their cultural heritage.

The prominence of clans was also of particular interest. The young people were for the most part very knowledgeable about the clan and kinship system, but this knowledge was mostly theoretical. Clan and kinship relationships did not feature in their everyday lives. In fact, some of them only became aware of which clan they belonged in their late teens or early 20s. They were anxious to distance themselves from their parents' and grandparents' generations in terms of the importance they place on clans. While the usefulness of a kinship system was acknowledged, especially for individuals in a time of need, they had rarely if at all experienced a need for assistance which had forced them to call on their clan. It is also worth remembering that the clan networks are not as strong in Australia as they were in Somalia, so there are limits to what can be achieved using these networks.

Gen 1.5 Somalis were aware of a disruption of their social capital due to their flight from Somalia. Although their families established and re-established networks here in Melbourne, they were conscious that they had lost their 'standing' in society. Some of them spoke about how their parents had created 'another Somalia' in Melbourne (perhaps evidence of the contention that Somalis in Melbourne are a very inward looking community), but how they felt locked out of this community, and thus had experienced a second rupture because they cannot or will not access the refugee networks their parents established. At the same time, many of the respondents felt that they were not able to take part fully in mainstream Australian society. Their descriptions echo the scholarly accounts of Gen 1.5 the world over: They are not fully integrated into their host countries' societies, nor their parents' communities and networks.

The young people described different strategies to enable them to move between the different spheres of their lives, most notably in their interactions with their parents and with the mainstream Australian community. However, many noted that this was challenging. They felt the burden of competing expectations and struggled to integrate their contested identities. In general, this age bracket (adolescence to young adulthood) is noted for being a challenging life period in terms of identity expression. Gen 1.5 Somali Australians are faced with compounded difficulty in this phase due to their visible minority status, multiple pressures from within their community, the increased scrutiny on their actions by outsiders, and other pressures brought to bear on them.

Somalis have been characterised as violent in both academic literature and the popular media. Various reasons have been advanced for this assessment including that violence is a Somali-specific character trait, the clan system, the harsh environment of Somalia, and due to outside political and military intervention in Somalia. However, my analysis does not support the contention that the ongoing violence Somalia is the inevitable enactment of ancient tribal allegiances. This illustrates the danger of ideological discourse — that false ideologies (or, at least, reductive and over-simplistic ones) become consolidated and permeate the identities of the individuals or collective.

The young people were able to detail acts of brutality that had taken place in Somalia and told stories of friends whose brothers, uncles and fathers had disappeared or been shot. Their reflections on overt violence, however, were almost exclusively located in Somalia. However, the study uncovered a number of examples of covert violence that affected the Somali community in Melbourne deeply. Perhaps chief among these was the closure of official channels through which remittances could be sent to Somalia. There is inherent violence in stopping the flow of money to a vulnerable population. This decision selectively victimised certain members of the population, and the Somali Australian community was powerless to act and defend the interests of their family and kin still in Somalia.

The young people offered many reflections on the sorts of violence that face them on a daily basis. These included problematic relationships with law enforcement, difficulty gaining adequate representation if they were in trouble with the law and the problem of absent or disengaged father figures. There was a notable difference in the way that young men and young women conceived of violence, with the men stressing issues with the police, and women focusing on intimate partner violence.

There have been many accusations against Victoria Police regarding their racial profiling of young African Australian males. It is clear that young male African Australians are much more likely to be stopped by members of the police force with no grounds. Their representation in crime statistics is also higher than the rest of the population, but not by as much as has been reported in various forms of the media.

Because of the perception of and perpetuation by the media, when violence does occur in the Somali Australian community, it appears to be subject to much more scrutiny than when it occurs in a mainstream setting. Many of the respondents pointed out that violence occurs in all communities, but that when it happens in a Muslim community and specifically in the Somali community, it is documented and disseminated broadly. This leads to an over-representation of Somali males (and Muslim males more broadly) being linked to violence and violent acts which in turn reinforces the notion that they are violent people.

The study uncovered no evidence to suggest that this generation of Somalis is more likely to engage in violent behaviour than the average Australian of the same age. The young people were dismissive of the idea that the Somali community in Melbourne poses a real threat. Instead, they believe that the danger has been overestimated for various reasons. Some pointed out that it is difficult to identify Somalis from other dark-skinned Africans, and some people might jump to conclusions about the identity of offenders. Others believe that the negative reportage about their community is purely to sell newspapers and attract TV viewers. Still others pointed out that there is a natural human need to have something to fear, and that, unfortunately, for many people, their community filled that need.

◊

Gen 1.5 Somali Australians are an exceptional group of young people. Their ways of being in the world displayed great courage, and agility in managing the many and competing pressures they face.

They spoke at length about the importance of Islam in their lives. I had previously thought of Islam as an organisational force for configuring social relations and cultural expectations. However, the young people also discussed their personal relationship with Allah in great detail. They believed that Islam was a force that improved them and encouraged them to strive to be better people. They also noted similarities between Islamic values and mainstream Australian values. Some stated that there are universal values of good and that all religions aspire to these. Their personal faith was strong and appeared to be the result of deep consideration rather than simply following the cultural and religious practices of their parents.

For the young people interviewed, religion, culture and ethnicity were important parts of their self-described identity. They shared many stories about how this identity had put them in risky, uncomfortable, or unsafe positions. But they also described their pride in their identity and the way they present themselves to the outside world.

All preliminary research pointed to the clans being a crucial aspect of Somali identity. Indeed, the older Somali Australians I spoke with highlighted the clan system as a valuable categorising and organising factor in their lives. The younger people were in some cases very dismissive of the clans and professed not to know or care much about them. However, they were very eager to talk about the clans amongst themselves in focus groups and with me in longer interviews. Some were anxious to distance themselves from the clan system in their lives in Australia. This was despite the fact that they were clearly well informed about the history of the clans and the way they operate both in Somali and in Australia. It is unclear why they professed such disinterest in the clan system, despite having an intimate working knowledge of the functions of clan allegiances. After consideration there seem to be two possible answers. Firstly, I believe that Gen 1.5 is deliberately trying to put distance between their way of life and their parents' (and grandparents'). Secondly, it is possible that the young people associated the clan system with the widespread negative perception of Somalis and therefore did not wish to identify with it. More research into this area would be instructive.

While it is not unusual for migrants to value education highly, it was surprising that education was a distinguishing factor for the young people's identities and something they believe sets the Somalis apart from other African communities in Melbourne. The respondents are active agents in their choices, and many have mapped out professional trajectories for themselves. All of them were very aware of the hardships their parents had faced in order to reach Australia and make a new life here. Some spoke directly about owing a debt to their parents and their wish to repay this debt by studying hard and trying to 'make something' of their lives.

It was also very interesting to observe how Somali Australians in general seem to set themselves apart from other communities, historically and but also in their daily lives in Melbourne. They have traditionally considered themselves distinct from others, based for example on their direct (mythical) connection to the prophet Muhammad. In their daily lives, they believe their interpretation and practice of Islam is different from other Muslim groups in Australia. They also believe their focus on education sets them apart from other migrant groups as described above. However, this conviction (along with the older generations' preference to rely on clan and kinship networks) may have contributed to theirs being a very insular and inward-looking community. While it emphasises the strength of their own networks, it has also served as a deterrent to individuals from accessing services which might be helpful. These include welfare services, social services which might promote cohesion with other community groups and medical and financial services.

It is also important to highlight the fragmented nature of the Somali community in Melbourne. This has been found elsewhere in Somali communities living abroad, but is not a universal feature of Somali diasporic communities (Al-Sharmani 2007; Horst 2007). It is often attributed to the clan system, which, it is argued, prevents Somalis from presenting a united front and may disadvantage them in their mission to seek resources, or begin community projects. While I agree that the clan system is to some degree responsible for this, it is possible that the social landscape for Somalis in Melbourne mirrors the social landscape in Somalia, which has been fragmented for many decades. This fragmentation has thwarted attempts to create a sense of Somali unity many times and will perhaps continue to do so. Additionally, my argument above that Somalis see themselves as different and set themselves apart from other minority groups and the mainstream community may also serve to be instructive. It is possible that the same fragmentation exists within the community, that small, insular and inward looking factions have been created. In this way, this insularity may have been split along other lines within the community to further reinforce the fragmentation which has been commented on by so many authors.

A further unexpected finding was the sense of respect that the males accord females in Somali culture. This is highly unusual with regard to the stereotypical expectations of Muslim gender relations, and indeed, some of the young women pointed out that they were frustrated with their Muslim (non-Somali) friends and acquaintances for the way that they submitted to the males in their lives. Both men and women described the inner strength of Somali women and the way that in Australia, many women are 'head of the household'. This is, they believed in contrast to other Muslim families, where children report to their fathers and are disciplined by them. Some women described how their mothers had successfully sought divorce as evidence of women's strength and their ability to be masters of their own destiny. While the participants talked about the pride that Somali women possess and their strong sense of self, both in Somalia and abroad, significant changes have been brought about by the migration experience. Women are experiencing freedom that they were less likely to experience in Somalia and taking advantage of the many opportunities that living in the western world affords. However, this upheaval has had a marked effect on Somali men, with some reporting feelings of alienation and anxiety about their new, less-defined gender roles.

A final unexpected finding relates to the disparity between the community belief that females outperform males in terms of educational achievement. The available census data does not support this; in fact, it quite clearly contradicts it. There seemed to be a universal consensus within the Somali community that young women are more studious than young men. It was clear that being more studious matched the parental and cultural expectations of young women. It was seen as a sign that young women are more mature and better able to manage the requirements of the outside world. The respondents reported that there is a disjuncture between the expectations that parents have of their sons and the tools they equip them with to succeed. In particular, the young women argued that because there are lower expectations of Somali boys to help around the house, and be involved in family life, they are less equipped to apply themselves to study and persevere with their education.

◊

This project has suggested many avenues for further research. It would be instructive to examine the disjuncture between the perceived educational achievement of females and the way this is contrasted to a perceived under-achievement of males within the community more closely. An examination of census data and the tracking of trends in this area would be particularly interesting taking into account the latest census data.

Secondly, deeper engagement with Somali Australians about what they believe constitutes violence, and gendered differences in this perception would be timely, particularly in the current climate of a renewed focus on domestic violence. This study has raised many questions about what Somali men and women consider violence to mean, and if measures are to be taken to address violence against women and children, it is crucial to understand the different perceptions men and women have of violence.

Thirdly, an investigation into the collection, compilation and publication of crime statistics in Victoria and a comprehensive examination of the issues around racial profiling allegedly carried out by police may alleviate public concerns about specific ethnic groups and help to reduce media hyperbole and scaremongering. This would certainly benefit the young people who participated in this study and improve their wellbeing.

It would also be interesting to carry out more targeted research into what effects media representation has on communities such as Somali Australians. While many authors have shown that the overrepresentation of particular groups in the media can lead to poor settlement, economic and mental health outcomes, it would be useful to see more information about how this occurs, and how to address this issue.

Finally, further research into what this study identified as a tendency within the Somali community in Melbourne to look inward, and to be quite insular in their efforts to overcome problems they face would be beneficial. Such research might discover ways of encouraging them to access outside services instead of relying solely on their own networks. It should be possible to target services to better meet the needs of Somalis in Melbourne, and to educate service providers in some of the specific characteristics of the community in order to achieve better social, financial, and medical outcomes. Similarly, such a project would require deeper engagement with members of the community to better understand their needs and the way they might access services, but it could also educate the Somali community about the existence of external support networks which are there to assist them.

◊

I was deeply affected by my engagement with Gen 1.5 Somalis Australians. I have often wondered about the hierarchy of migrants as described by some of the respondents. Do they feel that they are at the lower end of some scale because of the relatively small numbers of refugees from Somalia, or is it because there are too many differences that need to be bridged between Somali culture and Australian culture? What does the future of the Somali community in Australia look like?

I am reminded of an anecdote told to me at a multicultural forum I attended at the Immigration Museum. There had been a call to migrant and refugee communities to donate some culturally significant artefacts for an exhibition, which were then to be kept as documented evidence of the different cultural groups residing in Melbourne. I asked the organiser whether she had reached out to the Somali community in Melbourne, as in my view, they would have very interesting artefacts and information to contribute. She told me that she had done so numerous times, but although they were very polite and at first seemed interested, the interest quickly waned. She said she had the feeling that they were 'too busy looking forward to look back'.

It seems that the Melbourne Somali community has yet to attain a safe cultural space in which they can celebrate their heritage in the knowledge that others will accord them respect rather than suspicion. Given the current political climate, and the demonstrated disparity between the expression of young Somali identity in Melbourne and the dominant representations of them, it seems that further research in this area might become increasingly relevant.

Bibliography

Abdullahi, Mohamed Diriye. 2001. *Culture and Customs of Somalia.* London: Greenwood Press.

Affi, Ladan. 2005. "Domestic conflict in the diaspora - Somali women asylum seekers and refugees in Canada." In *Somalia- The Untold story: The War Through the Eyes of Somali Women*, edited by Judith Gardner and Judy El Bushra. London: Pluto Press.

Aidid, Mohammed Farrah, and Satya Pal Ruhela. 1994. *Somalia: From the Dawn of Civilization to the Modern Times*. New Delhi: Vikas Publishing House.

Akbarzadeh, Shahram, and B Smith. 2005. *The Representation of Muslims and Islam and the Media (The Age and Herald Sun).* Monash University (Melbourne).

Al-Sharmani, Mulki. 2007. "Diasporic Somalis in Cairo: The Poetics and Practices of Soomaalinimo." In *From Mogadisho to Dixon: The Somali Diaspora in a Global Context*, edited by A. Kusow and SR. Bjork. Trenton, New Jersey: Red Sea.

Ali, Ayaan Hirsi. 2010. *Nomad.* New York: Free Press.

Ali, Emua, and Crispin Jones. 2000. *Meeting the Educational Needs of Somali Pupils in Camden Schools.* University of London (Institute of Education).

Alia, Valerie, and Simone Bull. 2005. *Media and Ethnic Minorities*. Edinburgh: Edinburgh University Press.

Althoff, Andrea. 2006. "Religious Identites of Latin American Immigrants in Chicago: Preliminary Findings from Field Research " Religion and Culture Web Forum.

Aly, Waleed. 24 September 2013. *Concern over Madrassas in Australia.* Radio National.

Amr, Hady, and Elizabeth Ferris. 19 September 2010. *Displacement in the Muslim World.* The Brookings Institution. http://www.brookings.edu/papers/2009/0216_displacement_amr.aspx

Amster, Ellen J. 2013. *Medicine and the Saints: Science, Islam and the Colonial Encounter in Morocco 1877-1956*. Austin: University of Texas Press.

An-Na'im, Abdullahi Ahmed. 2010. *Islam and the Secular State*. Boston: Harvard University Press.

Australian Bureau of Statistics. 2011. *Census 2011.* Australian Bureau of Statistics (Canberra).

---. 2016. *Census 2016.* Australian Bureau of Statistics (Canberra).

Australian Government. 2009. *Afghan Cameleers in Australia.* Australian Government (Canberra). http://www.australia.gov.au/about-australia/australian-story/afghan-cameleers

---. 2013. *Information Paper - Humanitarian Program.* Canberra: Deparment of Immigration and Border Protection.

---. 2014. "The People of Australia – Australia's Multicultural Policy." Australian Government. Accessed Accessed 6 December 2014. https://www.dss.gov.au/our-responsibilities/settlement-and-multicultural-affairs/publications/the-people-of-australia-australias-multicultural-policy

Australian Human Rights Commission. 2009. *African Australians: A report on human rights and social inclusion issues. Discussion Paper.* AHRC (Sydney).

Aw-Ossman, Farah. 2009. "Somali Youth: Stop the Violence." *Aw-Osman* (blog). http://aw-osman.blogspot.co.uk/2009/08/somali-youth-stop-violence.html

Bailey, Paul. 2015. *Guidance for Working with Children and Young People who are vulnerable to the messages of Radicalisation and Extremism.* Merton Safeguarding Children Board (London Borough of Merton).

Barrows, Leland Conley. 2008. "Somalia." In *Oxford Encyclopedia of the Modern world,* edited by Peter N. Stearns. Oxford Oxford University Press.

Barton, David, and Karin Tusting. 2005. *Beyond communities of practice. Language, power, and social context.* Cambridge: Cambridge University Press.

Battersby, Lucy. 2015. "Veil lifts on daily abuse faced by Australian Muslims." *The Sydney Morning Herald,* 2 December, 2015.

Bayly, Cristopher. 1999. "The Second British Empire." In *The Oxford History of the British Empire,* 1-22. Oxford: Oxford University Press.

BBC News Australia. 16 March 2015. "Australian counter-terror police 'stopping 400 per day'." *BBC News,* 16 March 2015. Accessed Accessed 22 March 2015. http://www.bbc.com/news/world-australia-31900876

Besteman, Catherine. 1999. *Unraveling Somalia: Race, Violence and the Legacy of Slavery.* Philadelphia: University of Pennsylvania Press.

Bigelow, Martha. 2010. "Researching and Educating Somali Immigrant and Refugee Youth." *Language Learning* 60 (1): 147-156.

Birman, Dina, Edison Trickett, and Natalia Bacchus. 2001. *Somali Refugee Youth in Maryland: Needs Assessment.* Maryland Department of Human Resources. (Maryland).

Black, Donald, and Albert Reiss. 1970. "Police Control of Juveniles." *American*

Sociological Review 35: 63-77.

Borzykowski, Brian. 2009. "Canada in 2020 (Education): The kids who fell between the cracks." *Canadian Business*, 2009. Accessed 22 December 2015. http://www.canadianbusiness.com/business-strategy/canada-in-2020-education-the-kids-who-fell-between-the-cracks/

Bourdieu, Pierre. 1985. "The social space and the genesis of groups." *Social Science Information* 24: 195-220.

---. 1986. "The forms of capital." In *Handbook of Theory and Research for the Sociology of Education* edited by J.E Richardson, 241-258. New York: Greenwood.

Bourdieu, Pierre, and Loic Wacquant. 1992. *An Invitation to Reflexive Sociology*. Chicago: University of Chicago Press.

Brenner, Louis. 1993. "Constructing Muslim Identities in Mali." In *Muslim Identity and Social Change in Sub-Sahara Africa*, edited by L Brenner, 59-78. London: Hurst & Company.

British Council. 2007. *Raising the attainment of Pakistani, Bangladeshi, Somali and Turkish heritage pupils.* British Council (London).

Brunson, Rod K, and Ronald Weitzer. 2009. "Police Relations with Black and White Youths in Different Urban Neighborhoods." *Urban Affairs Review* 44 (6): 858-885.

Buchanan, ZE, HM Abu-Rayya, E Kashima, SJ Paxton, and DL Sam. 2018. "Perceived discrimination, language proficiencies, and adaptation: Comparisons between refugee and non-refugee immigrant youth in Australia." *International Journal of Intercultural Relations* 63: 105-112.

Burke, Peter J 2003. "Introduction." In *Advances in Identity Theory and Research*, edited by Peter J Burke, Timothy J Owens, Richard T Serpe and Thoits Peggy A, 1-7. New York: Kluwer Academic/Plenum Publishers.

Burnside, Julian. 2013. Asylum Seekers and Refugees. Speech given at launch of UN Report Card 2013, Melbourne: United Nations Association of Australia.

Cady, Duane L. 2006. "Violence." In *Encyclopedia of Philosophy*, edited by Donald M. Borchert. Detroit: Macmillan Reference USA.

Carter, David. 2006. *Dispossession, Dreams& Diversity, Issues in Australian Studies, Australia.* Australia: Pearson Education

Cassanelli, Lee. 1982. *The Shaping of Somali Society: Reconstructing the History of a Pastoral People, 1500-1900*. Philadelphia: Philadelphia University Press.

Castles, Stephen, and Mark Miller. 2008. *The Age of Migration: International Population Movements in the Modern World.* Hampshire: Palgrave Macmillan.

Centre for Multicultural Youth. 2014. *Fair and Accurate? Migrant and Refugee Young People, Crime and the Media.* Centre for Multicultural Youth (Carlton, Melbourne).

Chapin Metz, Helen. 1992. *Somalia: A Country Study.* Federal Research Division Library of Congress (Washington).

Chen, Carolyn. 2002. "The Religious Varieties of Ethnic Presence: A Comparison Between a Taiwanese Immigrant Buddhist Temple and an Evangelical Christian Church." *Sociology of Religion* 59 (3): 259-286.

Chen, S, and R Schweitzer. 2019. "The Expereince of Belonging in Youth from Refugee Backgrounds: A Narrative Perspective." *Journal of Child and Family Studies* 28: 1977-1990.

Clarke, Simon. 2008. "Culture and Identity." In *The SAGE Handbook of Cultural Analysis*, edited by Tony Bennet and John Frow. Thousand Oaks, California: SAGE Publishing.

Clyne, Michael, and Sandra Kipp. 1999. *Pluricentric languages in a immigrant context*. Berlin: Mouton de Gruyter.

Colaguori, Claudio. 2010. "Symbolic Violence and the Violation of Human Rights: Continuing the Sociological Critique of Domination " *International Journal of Criminology and Sociological Theory* 3 (2): 388-400.

Commonwealth of Australia. 2018. *Somalia-born Community Information Summary.* Department of Home Affairs (Australian Bureau of Statistics).

Cottle, Simon. 2004. *The Racist Murder of Stephen Lawrence: Media Performance and Public Transformation.* London: Praeger.

Cummings, Chris. 4 April 2015. "Westpac Bank in Australia Ceases Somali Remittances." *American Banker*, 4 April 2015.

Darboe, Kebba. 2003. "New Immigrant in Minnesota: The Somali Immigration and Assimilation." *Journal of Developing Societies* 19 (4): 458-472.

Das, Veena, and Arthur Kleinman. 2011. "Introduction." In *Remaking a World: Violence, Social Suffering and Recovery*, edited by Veena Das, Arthur Kleinman, Margaret Lock, Mamphela Ramphele and Pamela Reynolds. Berkely, California: University of California Press.

DeShaw, Pamela J. August 2006. "Use of the Emergency Department by Somali Immigrants and Refugees." *Minnesota Medicine.*

Dixon, Travis L., and Charlotte L. Williams. 2015. "The Changing Misrepresentation of Race and Crime on Network and Cable News." *Journal of Communication* 65 (1): 24-39.

Dominguez Diaz, Marta. 2015. *Women in Sufism: Female Religiosities in a Transnational Order*. New York: Routledge.

Donovan, Samantha. 2013. "Victoria Police settles racial profiling case." *ABC News*, February 18, 2013. Accessed Accessed 4 January 2016. http://www.abc.net.au/news/2013-02-18/police-agree-to-new-procedures-to-combat-racism/4524770

Dwyer, Claire. 1998. "Contested Identities: Challenging Dominant Representations of Young British Muslim Women." In *Cool Places: Geographies of Youth Cultures*, edited by T Skelton and G Valentine. London: Routledge.

Eagleton, Terry, and Pierre Bourdieu. 1992. "Doxa and Common Life." *New Left Review* 191 (111-121).

Ebaugh, Helen R, and Janet S Chafetz. 2000. *Religion and the New Immigrants: Continuities and Adaptations in Immigrant Congregations*. California: AltaMira Press.

Engel, Robin. 2003. "Explaining Suspects' Resistance and Disrespect toward Police." *Journal of Criminal Justice* 31: 475-92.

Esposito, John L. 2008. "Introduction: Islam in Asia in the Twenty-First Century." In *Asian Islam in the 21st Century*, edited by John L. Esposito, John O. Voll and Osman Bakar. New York: Oxford University Press.

Farah, Nuruddin. 1986. *Maps*. New York: Arcade Publishing.

---. 1998. *Secrets*. New York: Arcade Publishing.

---. 2004. *Links*. New York City: Riverhead Books.

---. 2007. *Knots* New York City: Riverhead Books.

Feher, Shoshana 1998. "From the Rivers of Babylon to the Valleys of Los Angeles:The Exodus and Adaptation of Iranian Jews." In *Gatherings in Diaspora: Religious Communities and the New Immigration*, edited by R.Stephen Warner and Judith G. Wittner, 71-94. Philadelphia: Temple University Press.

Fennelly, Katherine, and Nicole Palasz. 2003. "English Language Proficiency of Immigrants and Refugees in the Twin Cities Metropolitan Area 41." *International Migration* 41 (5): 93-125.

Ferguson, R. Brian. 2004. "Tribal Warfare." In *Violence in War and Peace*, edited by Nancy Scheper-Hughes and Phillippe Bourgois, 69-73. Oxford, UK: Blackwell Publishing.

Fishman, Shira. February 16 2010. *Community-Level Indicators of Radicalization: A Data and Methods Task Force.* U.S. Department of Homeland Security (University of Maryland).

Foner, Nancy. 1979. *Jamaica Farewell: Jamaican Immigrants in London* London: Routledge & Kegan Paul.

---. 1997. "The immigrant family: Cultural legacies and cultural changes." *The International Migration Review* 31 (4): 961-974.

Foucault, Michel. 1998 [1976]. *The History of Sexuality, Volume One: The Will to Knowledge.* Translated by Random House. London: Penguin.

Frodesen, Jan. 2002. "At what price success?: The academic writing development of a generation 1.5 "latecomer." " *The CATESOL Journal* 14 (1): 191-206.

Garcia-Muñoz, Teresa, and Shoshana Neuman. 2013. "Bridges or buffers? Motives behind Immigrants' Religiosity." *IZA Journal of Migration* 2 (23).

Garner, Judith, and Judy El Bushra. 2005. *Somalia - The Untold Story: The War Through the Eyes of Somali Women.* London: Pluto Press.

Gebrewold, Belachew. 2009. *Anatomy of Violence: Understanding the Systems of Conflict and Violence in Africa.* Surrey, England: Ashgate Publishing Limited.

Gellner, Ernst. 1993. "Marxism and Islam: Failure and Success." In *Power-Sharing Islam?*, edited by A Tamimi. London: Liberty for Muslim World Publications.

Ghauri, MJ, and S Umber. 2019. "Exploring the Nature of Representation of Islam and Muslims in the Australian Press." *SAGE Open.* https://doi.org/https://doi.org/10.1177/2158244019893696.

Gibson, Margaret A 1988. *Accommodation Without Assimilation: Sikh Immigrants in an American High School.* Ithaca, NY: Cornell University Press.

Goffman, Erving. 1963. *Stigma: Notes on the Management of Spoiled Identity.* Englewood Cliffs, NJ: Prentice-Hall.

Gourevitch, Philip. 2004. "We Wish to Inform you the Tomorrow we will be Killed with our Families: Stories from Rwanda." In *Violence in War and Peace*, edited by N Scheper-Hughes and P Bourgois, 136-142. Oxford, UK: Blackwell Publishing.

Griffiths, David. 2002. *Somali and Kurdish Refugees in london: New Identities in the Diaspora.* Burlington: Ashgate.

Gundel, Joakim. 2002. "The Migration–Development Nexus: Somalia Case Study " *International Migration* 40 (5): 255-281.

Haakonsen, Jan M., and Hassan K. Keynan, eds. 1995. *Somalia after UNOSOM: Proceedings from a Conference Held in Oslo, 9-10 March 1995*. Oslo: Norwegian Red Cross.

Haddad, Yvonne Y, and Adair T Lummis. 1987. *Islamic Values in the United States: A Comparative Study*. New York: Oxford University.

Haffejee, B. 2015. "African refugee youths' stories of surviving trauma and transition in U.S. Public schools." *Journal of Muslim Mental Health* 9 (1): 3-23.

Hage, Ghassan. 1998. *White Nation: Fantasies of White Supremacy in a Multicultural Society*. New South Wales: Pluto.

---. 2003. *Against Paranoid Nationalism*. Sydney: Pluto Press.

Haile-Michael, Daniel, and Maki Issa. 2015. *The More Things Change, The More they Stay the Same: Racial profiling across Melbourne.* Flemington and Kensington Community Legal centre (Kensington).

Hall, Stuart. 1995. "Fantasy, identity, politics." In *Cultural remix: theories of politics and the popular*, edited by Erica Carter, James Donald and Judith Squires, 63-69. London: Lawrence & Wishart.

Hammond, Phillip E. 1988. "Religion and the Persistence of Identity." *Journal for the Scientific Study of Religion* 27 (1): 1-11.

Hansen, Peter. 2008. "Circumcising Migration: Gendering Return Migration among Somalilanders " *Journal of Ethnic and Migration Studies* 34 (7): 1109-1125.

Harding, Jenny, Andrew Clarke, and Adrian Chappell. 2007. *Family Matters: Intergenerational Conflict in the Somali Community.* Department of Applied Social Sciences (London Metropolitan University).

Harzig, Christiane, Dirk Hoerder, and Donna Gabaccia. 2009. *What is Migration History?* Cambridge, UK: Polity Press.

Hassig, Susan. 1997. *Cultures of the World: Somalia*. Vol. New York. Times Editions.

Hatoss, Anikó, and Henk Huijser. 2010. "Gendered Barriers to Educational Opportunities: Resettlement of Sudanese Refugees in Australia " *Gender and Education* 22 (2): 147-160.

Herberg, Will. 1955. *Protestant-Catholic-Jew: An Essay in American Religious Sociology*. New York: Doubleday and Company.

---. 1960. *Protestant - Catholic - Jew: An Essay in American Religious Sociology*. Garden City, New York: Anchor Books.

Herger Boyle, Elizabeth, and Ahmed Ali. 2010. "Culture, Structure, and the Refugee Experience in Somali Immigrant Family Transformation." *International Migration Review* 48 (1): 46-56.

Hesse, Brian. 2010. "The Myth of 'Somalia'." *Journal of Contemporary African Studies* 28 (3): 247-259.

Hewitt, John. 1989. *Dilemmas of the American Self*. Philadelphia: Temple University Press.

---. 2003. *Self and Society: A Symbolic Interactionist Social Psychology*. Boston: Allyn and Bacon.

Ho, Christina. 2007. "Muslim Women's New Defenders: Women's Rights, Nationalism and Islamophobia in Contemporary Australia." *Women's Studies International Forum* 30: 290-298.

Hobbes, Thomas. 1996. *Leviathan.* edited by Richard Tuck. Cambridge: Cambridge University Press.

Horst, Cindy. 2007. "The Somali Diaspora in Minneapolis: Expectations and Realities." In *From Mogadishu to Dixon: The Somali Diaspora in a Global Context*, edited by A. Kusow and SR. Bjork. Trenton, New Jersey: Red Sea.

Houlihan, Liam. 2008. "Fears our crime being imported." *Sunday Herald Sun*, 9 March, 2008.

Hughes, Gabrielle. 2013. "Somali Refugees' Views on Education in Melbourne, Australia: Implications for Identity Formation and Public Policy." Masters, School of Social and Political Sciences, The University of Melbourne

Hurd, Noelle, Marc Zimmerman, and Yange Xue. 2009. "Negative adult influences and the protective effects of role models: A study with urban adolescents." *Journal of Youth and Adolescents* 38 (6): 777-789.

Hurh, Won Moo , and Kwang Chung Kim. 1990. "Religious Participation of Korean Immigrants in the United States." *Journal for the Scientific Study of Religion* 29: 19-34.

Hurst, Yolander, James Frank, and Sandra Browning. 2000. "The Attitudes of Juveniles towards the Police." *Policing* 23 (37-53).

Huster, Kim A. . 2011. "Suspended Between Lanugages: Stories from the Biliterate Lives of Hmong Generation 1.5 University Women." PhD, University of Pennsylvania.

Hyndman, Jennifer. 1999. "A Post-Cold War Geography of Forced Migration in Kenya and Somalia." *The Professional Geographer* 51 (1): 104-114.

Ibrahim, Mohamed. 2010. "Somalia and Global Terrorism: A Growing Connection?" *Journal of Contemporary African Studies* 28 (3): 283-295.

Ingiriis, Mohamed Haji. 2010. "Somalia: From finest to failed state." *Africa Review*, 28 September, 2010. Accessed Accessed 10 January 2016. http://www.africareview.com/Special-Reports/The-rise-of-dictatorship-in-Somalia/-/979182/1019576/-/tujl4q/-/index.html

Institute for Middle East Understanding. 2009. *Background Briefings: Palestine (2006-2009).* Institute for Middle East Understanding (California). http://imeu.net/news/background-briefings.shtml

International Religious Freedom (2010): Annual Report to Congress. 26 August 2010. United States Commission on International Religious Freedom (Washington, DC).

Jefferess, David. 2008. *Resistance: Culture, Liberation and Transformation.* Toronto: University of Toronto Press.

Jensen, T, E Skårdalsmo, and K Fjermestad. 2014. "Development of mental health problems - a follow-up study of unaccompanied refugee minors." *Child and Adolescent Psychiatry and Mental Health* 8 (1): 29.

Johnson, Laurie M. 1993. *Thucydides, Hobbes, and the Interpretation of Realism.* Dekalb: Northern Illinois Press.

Kabir, Nahid. 2006. "Representation of Islam and Muslims in the Australian Media, 2001-2005." *Journal of Muslim Minority Affairs* 26 (3): 313-328.

Kahin, Mohammed. 1997. *Educating Somali Children in Britain.* London: Trentham Books.

Kapteijns, Lidwien. 2013. *Clan Cleansing in Somalia: The Ruinous Turn of 1991.* Pennsylvania: University of Pennsylvania Press.

Keating, Maree, and Bonnie Simons. 2008. *Somali students in VET- some factors influencing pathways.* Equity Research Centre.

Khamis, Noor. 2015. "Kenya Arrests Five Over Deadly al Shabaab Attack on University." *Reuters*, 2015. Accessed Accessed 11 January 2016. http://www.newsweek.com/five-arrested-kenya-al-shabaab-attack-319666

Kibria, Nazli. 1993. *Family Tightrope: The Changing Lives of Vietnamese Americans*. Princeton: Princeton University Press.

Kleist, Nauja. 2010. "Negotiating Respectable Masculinity: Gender and Recognition in the Somali Diaspora." *African Diaspora* 3: 185-206.

Knafla, Louis A. 2004. "Violence." In *Europe, 1450 to 1789: Encyclopedia of the Early Modern World*, edited by Jonathan Dewald. New York: Charles Scribner's Sons.

Kurien, Prema. 1998. "Becoming American by Becoming Hindu: Indian Americans Take Their Place at the Multicultural Table." In *Gatherings in Diaspora: Religious Communities and the New Immigration*, edited by R.S Warner and J.G Wittner, 37-70. Philadelphia: Temple University Press.

Kwon, Victoria H 2000. "Houston Korean Ethnic Church: An Ethnic Enclave." In *Religion and the New Immigrants: Continuities and Adaptations in Immigrant Congregations*, edited by H.R Ebaugh and J.S Chafetz, 109-123. California: AltaMira Press.

Laban Hinton, Alexander. 2004. "Why did you Kill?: The Cambodian Genocide and the Dark Side of Face and Honor." In *Violence in War and Peace*, edited by N Scheper-Hughes and P Bourgois, 157-168. Oxford, UK: Blackwell Publishing.

Langewiesche, William. 2009. "The Pirate Latitudes." *Vanity Fair*, 12-16.

Lee, Y, O Shin, and M Lim. 2012. "The psychological problems of North Korean adolescent refugees living in South Korea." *Psychiatry Investigation* 9 (3): 217.

Lewis, Ian M. 1955. *Peoples of the Horn of Africa: Somali, Afar, and Saho*. London: International African Institute.

---. 1961. *A Pastoral Democracy*. Munster: LIT Verlag.

---. 1994. *Blood and Bone: The Call of Kinship in Somali Society*. New Jersey: The Red Sea Press.

---. 2002. *A modern history of the Somali*. Ohio: Ohio University Press.

Lough, Richard. 2011. "Piracy ransom cash ends up with Somali militants." *Reuters*, 6 July 2011, 2011. Accessed Accessed 10 May 2015. http://uk.reuters.com/article/2011/07/06/uk-somalia-piracy-idUKTRE7652AW20110706

MacLellan, Nic. 2002. "The Pacific "Non-Solution"." *Pacific Journalism Review* 8: 145-154.

Maddison, Sarah. 2014. "Indigenous identity, 'authenticity' and the structural violence of settler colonialism." *Identities: Global Studies in Culture and Power* 20 (3): 288-303.

Manning, Peter. 2004. "Australians Imagining Islam." In *Muslims and the News Media*, edited by E Poole and J.E Richardson. London: I.B. Tauris Co.

Maynes, Mary Jo, Jennifer L. Pierce, and Barbara Laslett. 2008. *Telling Stories: The use of Personal Narratives in the Social Sciences and History*. London: Cornell University Press.

McGown, Rima. 1999. *Muslims in the Diaspora: The Somali Communities of London and Toronto*. Toronto: Toronto: University of Toronto Press.

McHoul, Alec, and Wendy Grace. 1993. *A Foucault Primer: Discourse Power and the Subject*. New York: New York University Press.

McMichael, Celia. 2003. "Memory and Resettlement: Somali Women in Melbourne and Emotional Wellbeing." PhD, University of Melbourne.

Media Watch. 24 March 2008. *Crime stats.* Australian Broadcasting Corporation. http://www.abc.net.au/mediawatch/transcripts/s2197803.htm

Mehmet, Murray. 2009. *Kurbet; The Albanian Experience.* Federation Square (Melbourne).

"Melbourne model turned jihadist Sharky Jama shot dead in Syria." 2015. *SBS News*, 2015. Accessed Accessed 11 May 2015. http://www.sbs.com.au/news/article/2015/04/15/melbourne-model-turned-jihadist-shot-dead-syria

Menkhaus, Ken. 2004. *Somalia: State Collapse and the Threat of Terrorism*. Oxford: Oxford University Press.

Miller, Pavla. 2004. "Gender and Education before and after Mass Schooling." In *A Companion to Gender History*, edited by Teresa Meade and Merry Wiesner-Hanks, 129-145. Malden: Blackwell.

Milovanovic, Selma. 16 March 2010. "Police racially abusing African youths: report." *The Age*, 16 March 2010.

Min, Pyong Gap , and Juan Ha Kim. 2002. *Religions in Asian America: Building Faith Communities*. California: AltaMira Press.

Moghissi, Haideh. 2006. *Muslim diaspora : gender, culture and identity*. London: Routledge.

Mohamed, Hamza. 2015. "The Other Side of Somalia's Pirates." *AlJazeera* 26 February 2015, 2015. Accessed Accessed 9 August 2015. http://www.aljazeera.com/indepth/features/2015/02/side-somalia-pirates-150225112818517.html

Moore, Nathaniel. 2007. "A Network of Assurance and Security: The Evolving Role of Clans in Somali Society." The Ohio State University.

Muchoki, Samuel M. 2013. "'[In Australia] what comes first are the women, then children, cats, dogs, followed by men': Exploring accounts of gender relations by men from the Horn of Africa." *Australasian Review of African Studies* 34 (2): 78-98.

Murphy, Kristina. 2011. "Fostering cooperation with the police: How do ethnic minorities in Australia respond to procedural justice-based policing?" *Australian and New Zealand Journal of Criminology* 44 (2): 235-257.

Noble, Greg, and Paul Taber. 2002. "On being Lebanese-Australian: hybridity, essentialism and strategy among Arabic-speaking youth." In *Arab Austra-*

lians today: citizenship and belonging, edited by Ghassan Hage. Melbourne: Melbourne University Press.

Nolan, David, Karen Farquharson, Tim Marjoribanks, and Denis Muller. 2014. *The AuSud Media Project 2011 - 2013*. University of Melbourne (Centre for Advancing Journalism).

Nunn, Caitlin, Celia McMichael, Sandra M. Gifford, and Ignacio Correa-Velez. 2014. "I came to this country for a better life': factors mediating employment trajectories among young people who migrated to Australia as refugees during adolescence." *Journal of Youth Studies* 17 (9): 1205-1220.

Oakes, Dan. 2012. "African Youth Crime Concern." *The Age*, 2012.

Omar, A. Rashied. 2004. "Conflict and Violence." In *Encyclopedia of Islam and the Muslim World*, edited by Richard C. Martin. New York: Macmillan Reference USA.

Omar, Yusuf Sheikh. 2011. "Integration from Youth Perspectives: A Comparative Study of Young Somali Men in Melbourne and Minneapolis." PhD, Latrobe University.

Onyx, Jenny, and Paul Bullen. 2005 [1997]. *Measuring Social Capital in Five Communities in NSW: A Practitioner's Guide*. Coogee, NSW: Management Alternatives.

Oudenhoven, E. D. . 2006. "Caught in the middle: Generation 1.5 Latino students and English language learning at a community college." Loyola University of Chicago.

Oxfam Australia Media. 30 March 2015. *Westpac's closure of vital lifeline could be catastrophic for Somalia - Oxfam.* Oxfam Australia (https://www.oxfam.org.au/media/2015/03/westpacs-closure-of-vital-lifeline-could-be-catastrophic-for-somalia-oxfam/).

Oxfeld, Ellen. 1993. *Blood, Sweat, and Mahjong: Family Enterprise in an Overseas Chinese Community*. Ithaca: Cornell University Press.

Pankhurst, Richard. 1998. *The Ethiopians: A History*. Oxford, UK: Blackwell.

Passerini, Luisa. 2005. "Introduction." In *Memory and Totalitarianism*, edited by Luisa Passerini. London: Transaction Publishers.

Pavlish, Carol Lynn, Sahra Noor, and Joan Brandt. 2010. "Somali Immigrant Women and the American health Care System: Discordant Beliefs, Divergent Expectations, and Silent Worries." *Soc Sci Med* 71 (2): 353-361.

Perrie, Ashlie, and Binneh Minteh. 2014. *Home Grown Terrorism in the United States: Causes, Affiliations and Policy implications.* Rutgers University.

Peucker, Mario, Joshua Roose, and Shahram Akbarzadeh. 2014. "Muslim active citizenship in Australia: Socioeconomic challenges and the emergence of a Muslim elite." *Australian Journal of Political Science* 49 (2).

Phillips, Janet. 2007. Muslim Australians. *Parliamentary Library E-Brief.*

Phillips, Janet, and Michael Klapdor. 2010. *Migration to Australia since federation: a guide to the statistics.* Parliamentary Library (Canberra).

Piliavin, Irving, and Scott Briar. 1964. "Police Encounters with Juveniles." *American Journal of Sociology* 70: 206-214.

Pinchbeck, Ivy, and Margaret Hewitt. 1973. *Children in English Society, Vol. 2: From the Eighteenth Century to the Children Act, 1948*. London: Routledge & Kegan Paul.

Pinker, Steven. 2007. "A Hstory of Violence." *The New Republic*, 19 March.

Pittaway, Eileen, and Christana Muli. 2009. *We Have a Voice, Hear Us: Settlement Experiences of Refugees and Migrants from the Horn of Africa.* Centre for Refugee Research, UNSW and Horn of African Relief and Development Agency (Sydney).

Portes, Alejandro 1998. "Social capital: its origins and applications in modern sociology." *Annual Review of Sociology* 24 (1): 1-25.

Poynting, Scott, and Victoria Mason. 2006. "Tolerance, Freedom, Justice and Peace?: Britain, Australia and Anti-Muslim Racism since 11 September 2001." *Journal of Intercultural studies* 27 (4): 365-391.

Pregulman, Ally, and Emily Burke. 2012. *Homegrown Terrorism.* Center for Strategic & International Studies (Washington D.C.).

Prestage, Edgar. 1933. *The Portuguese Pioneers* London: A & C Black Ltd.

Ramsden, Robyn. 2008. "The Hope of Education: Somali Families and Social Connections." PhD, Faculty of Health, Medicine, Nursing and Behavioural Sciences, Deakin University.

Ramsden, Robyn, and Damien Ridge. 2012. "'It Was the Most Beautiful Country I Have Ever Seen': The Role of Somali Narratives in Adapting to a New Country." *Journal of Refugee Studies* 26 (2): 226-246.

Ramsden, Robyn, and Ann Taket. 2013. "Social Capital and Somali Families in Australia." *International Migration & Integration* 14 (1): 99-117.

Ray, Larry. 2011. *Violence and Society*. London: SAGE Publications.

Rayaprol, Aparna. 1997. *Negotiating Identities: Women in the Indian Diaspora.* Delhi: Oxford University Press.

Reech, Thokgor. 2012. "African Communities Confront Police over Crime Statistics." *The Gazelle*, 2012. Accessed Accessed 19 August 2015. https://ausudmediaproject.wordpress.com/2012/10/27/african-communities-confront-police-over-crime-statistics/

Refugee Council. 2021. "Statistics on boat arrivals and boat turnbacks." Refugee Council. Accessed 15 Feb 2021. https://www.refugeecouncil.org.au/asylum-boats-statistics/.

Refugees International. 2011a. "Iraq." Where We Work. Accessed Accessed 14 June 2012. http://www.refugeesinternational.org/where-we-work/middle-east

---. 2011b. "Sudan." Where We Work. Accessed Accessed 14 June 2012. http://www.refugeesinternational.org/where-we-work/africa/sudan

Renaldi, Erwin. 2020. "Melbourne Muslims feel 'unfairly tarnished' by reports linking them to rising COVID-19 cases." ABC News. Accessed 15 February 2021. https://www.abc.net.au/news/2020-07-15/muslims-melbourne-raising-concern-over-covid19-reports/12454846.

Riley, Philip. 2007. *Language, Culture and Identity: An Ethnolinguistic Perspective*. London: Continuum.

Rorty, Amelie. 1976. *The Identities of Persons*. Berkeley: University of California Press.

Roulstone, Allan, and Hannah Mason-Bish. 2013. *Disability, Hate Crime and Violence*. Oxon: Routledge.

Roy, Beth. 1999. *Bitters in the Honey: Tales of Hope and Disappointment across the Divides of Race and Time*. Fayetville, AR: University of Arkansas Press.

Rumbaut, Ruben G., and Kenji Ima. 1988. *The adaptation of Southeast Asian refugee youth. A comparative study. Final report to the Office of Resettlement.* San Diego State University (San Diego: Office of Refugee Resettlement).

Saeed, Abdullah. 2003. *Islam in Australia*. Sydney: Allen & Unwin.

---. 2004. *Muslim Australians: Their Beliefs, Practices and Institutions.* Australian Government (Canberra).

Said, Aden. 2005. *Banyule Community Health Service Somali Research Project.* Banyule City Council (Melbourne).

Said, Edward. 1978. *Orientalism*. New York: Pantheon Books.

Samatar, Ahmed. 1988. *Socialist Somalia: Rhetoric and Reality* London: Institue for African Alternatives Zed Books.

---. 1989. *The State and Rural Transformation in Northern Somalia.* Wisconsin: The University of Wisconsin Press.

Sarroub, Loukia. 2005. *All American Yemeni Girls*. Philadelphia: University of Pennsylvania Press.

Scheper-Hughes, Nancy, and Phillippe Bourgois. 2004. "Introduction: Making Sense of Violence." In *Violence in War and Peace*, edited by Nancy Scheper-Hughes and Phillippe Bourgois, 1-31. Oxford, UK: Blackwell Publishing.

Schliebs, Mark. 2015. "Ex-model Sharky Jama killded as Jihadi toll totals 20." *The Australian*, April 16, 2015, 2015.

Schubert, J. Daniel. 2008. "Suffering/symbolic violence." In *Pierre Bourdieu: Key Concepts*, edited by Michael James Grenfell, 179-184. Oxon: Routledge.

Sedgwick, Mark J.R. 1997. "Saudi Sufis: Compromise in the Hijaz, 1925-40." *Die Welt des Islams* 37 (3): 349-368.

Seidel, Peter, and Tamar Hopkins. 2013. "No one should be stopped by police just because they're black." *The Age*, February 19, 2013. Accessed Accessed 4 January 2016. http://www.theage.com.au/comment/no-one-should-be-stopped-by-police-just-because-theyre-black-20130218-2end5.html

Sen, Amartya. 2006. *Identity and Violence: The Illusion of Destiny*. New York: Norton.

Shand, Adam. 2013. "Madrassa lessons worry Somalis." *The Australian*, September 24, 2013, 43.

"Sharky Jama, Melbourne male model, reportedly killed fighting with Islamic State in Syria." 2015. *ABC News*, 2015. Accessed Accessed 13 May 2015. http://www.abc.net.au/news/2015-04-16/sharky-jama-dfat-will-not-confirm-reports-australian-model-death/6396112

Sheridan, Greg. 2013. "Policy Failure Creating a Monstrous Problem." *The Australian*, 2013, 32. Accessed Accessed 18 August 2014. http://www.theaustralian.com.au/opinion/columnists/policy-failure-creating-a-monstrous-problem/story-e6frg76f-1226659596004?nk=4de6cdbe93be040bb-4c3e7319d115db9

Shohat, Ella, and Stam Robert. 1994. *Unthinking Eurocentrism: Multiculturalism and the Media*. Routledge: London.

Sian, Katy, Ian Law, and S. Sayyid. 2012. *The Media and Muslims in the UK.* University of Leeds (Centre for Ethnicity and Racism Studies).

Smith, Janita. 2008. *Problem Gambling in New and Emerging Refugee Communities.* Centre for Culture, Ethnicity and Health (Melbourne).

Smith, Timothy L 1978. "Religion and Ethnicity in America." *American Historical Review* 83: 1155-1185.

Spaaij, Ramón. 2012. "Beyond the Playing Field: Experiences of Sport, Social Capital and Integration among Somalis in Australia." *Ethnic and Racial Studies* 35 (9): 1519-1538.

Spalek, Basia, and Alia Imtoual. 2007. "Muslim Communities and Counter-Terror Responces: "Hard" Approaches to Community Engagement in the UK and Australia." *Journal of Muslim Minority Affairs* 27 (2): 185-202.

Sporton, Deborah, Gill Valentine, and Katrina B Nielsen. 2006. "Post Conflict Identities: Affiliations and Practices of Somali Asylum Seeker Children." *Children's Geographies* 4: 203-217.

Stanton, Martin. 2003. *Somali on $5 a Day: A Soldier's Story*. New York: Presidio Press.

Stets, Jan E. 1995. "Role Identities and Person Identities: Gender Identity, Mastery Identity, and Controlling One's Partner." *Sociological Perspectives* 38 (2): 129-150.

Stone, Gregory P 1962. "Appearance and the Self." In *Human Behavior and Social Processes*, edited by Arnold M Rose, 86-118. Boston: Houghton Mifflin.

Sullivan, Kathleen. 2000. "Iglesia de Dios: An Extended Family." In *Religion and the New Immigrants: Continuities and Adaptations in Immigrant Congregations*, edited by Helen R Ebaugh and Janet S Chafetz, 141-151. California: AltaMira Press.

Swingewood, Alan. 2000. *A Short History of Sociological Thought*. 3rd edition ed. Basingstoke: Palgrave.

Taha, Mohaned, and Philippa McDonald. 2014. "'No-one sits next to me anymore': Australian Muslim women on how their lives have changed." *ABC News*, 2 October, 2014.

Taylor, Charles. 1989. *The Sources of the Self: The Making of the Modern Identity*. Cambridge, MA: Harvard University Press.

Taylor, Eric H., and Lisa S. Barton. 1994. *Southeast Asian Refugee English Proficiency & Education in Texas.* Texas Department of Human Services (Texas).

Thomas, William I. 1937. *Primitive Behaviour*. New York: McGraw-Hill.

Touval, Saadia. 1963. *Somali Nationalism: International Politics and the Drive for Unity in the Horn of Africa* Cambridge: Harvard University Press.

Van Tubergen, Frank, and Jorunn I. Sindradottir. 2011. "The Religiosity of Immigrants in Europe: A Cross-National Study." *Journal for the Scientific Study of Religion* 50 (2): 272-288.

Verini, James. 2015. "Escape or Die." *The New Yorker*, 2015. Accessed Accessed

10 May 2015. http://www.newyorker.com/magazine/2015/04/20/escape-or-die

Victoria Police. 2014. *Crime Statistics 2013/2014.* Melbourne Victoria Police.

Vryan, Kevin D, Patricia A Adler, and Peter Adler. 2003. "Identity." In *Handbook of Symbolic Interactionism*, edited by Larry T Reynolds and Nancy J Herman-Kinnery, 367-390. New York: AltaMira Press.

Wambua-Soi, Catherine. 2015. "Garissa: What has changed since Westgate?" *AlJazeera*, 5 April, 2015. Accessed Accessed 10 April 2015. http://www.aljazeera.com/blogs/africa/2015/04/garissa-changed-westgate-150405123032987.html

Warne-Smith, Drew, and Lauren Wilson. 6 August 2009. "Somali terror suspects 'new to mosque'." *The Australian*, 6 August 2009.

Warner, R. Stephen. 1998. "Immigration and Religious Communities in the United States." In *Gatherings in Diaspora: Religious Communities and the New Immigration*, edited by R. Stephen Warner and J udith G. Wittner, 3-34. Philadelphia: Temple University Press.

Warner, R. Stephen, and Judith G. Wittner. 1998. *Gatherings in Diaspora: Religious Communities and the New Immigration.* Philadelphia: Temple University Press.

Watson, James. 1977. *Between Two Cultures: Migrants and Minorities in Britain.* Oxford: Basil Blackwell.

Weinstein, Barbara. 2005. "History Without a Cause? Grand Narratives, World History, and the Postcolonial Dilemma." *Internationaal Instituut voor Sociale Geschiedenis* 50: 71-93.

Weitzer, Ronald, and Rod K Brunson. 2009. "Strategic responses to the police among inner-city youth." *The Sociological Quarterly* 50: 235-256.

Wendt, Alexander. 1999. *Social Theory of International Politics*. Cambridge: Cambridge University Press.

Wharton, Barrie. 2014. "Globalization, Islam and the struggle for cultural identity in contemporary Europe." RMIT, 14 October.

White, Rob, Santina Perrone, Carmel Guerra, and Rosario Lampugnani. 1999. *Somali Young People.* Australian Multicultural Foundation (Melbourne).

Williams, Allan. 2003. *Fact Sheet - Somalia.* Adult Migrant English Program.

Williams, Raymond Brady. 1988. *Religions of Immigrants from India and Pakistan: New Threads in the American Tapestry*. New York: Cambridge University Press.

Wilson, David. 2007. *Cities and Race: America's New Black Ghetto*. New York: Routledge.

Yang, Fenggang. 1999. *Chinese Christians in America: Conversion, Assimilation, and Adhesive Identities*. University Park: The Pennsylvania State University Press.

Yang, Fenggang, and Helen R Ebaugh. 2001. "Religion and Ethnicity Among New Immigrants: The Impact of Majority/Minority Status in Home and Host Countries." *Journal for the Scientific Study of Religion* 40 (3): 367-378.

Yazbeck Haddad, Yvonne, and Jane I. Smith. 2002. *Muslim Minorities in the West: Visible and Invisible*. California: Altamira Press.

Yuval-Davis, Nira. 2006. "Belonging and the Politics of Belonging." *Patterns of Prejudice* 40 (3): 197-214.

Zammit, Andrew. 16 April, 2015 2015. *Australian Foreign Fighters: Risks and Responses.* Lowy Institute (Sydney). http://www.lowyinstitute.org/publications/australian-foreign-fighters-risks-and-responses

www.ingramcontent.com/pod-product-compliance
Lightning Source LLC
LaVergne TN
LVHW020042110826
845155LV00029B/608